Rich Miller is President of Freedom in Christ Ministries – USA.

He was on staff with Campus Crusade for Christ from 1976 to 1993 and has traveled around the world in Christian missions work. During his years with Campus Crusade for Christ, he ministered to youth in America and trained other staff to work with youth; was a missionary to the Philippines where he was in charge of the ministry there; and traveled for a year with author and speaker, Josh McDowell.

Rich joined Freedom in Christ Ministries in 1993. He is passionate about revival of the Church in America, and has authored or co-authored twenty-five books and discipleship manuals, including *Freedom from Fear, Getting Anger Under Control, Breaking the Bondage of Legalism, Journey to Freedom* and the Freedom Discipleship Series. He is also author of *To My Dear Slimeball*, a youth-oriented version of the C. S. Lewis classic *The Screwtape Letters*.

Rich spearheaded the development of the volunteer-based Community Freedom Ministry strategy of FICM-USA and now oversees the development and growth of the online training institute, CFM University. He also serves as FICM International Chairman, helping oversee the integrity and expansion of the message and ministry of freedom around the world.

Rich earned a Bachelor of Science in meteorology at Penn State University (1976), a Master of Arts in Christian Apologetics from Simon Greenleaf University (1986), and received an additional Master of Arts in Christian Counseling from Luther Rice Seminary in Atlanta (2007).

Rich leads teaching seminars such as Breaking Free in Christ and Extreme Church Makeover (formerly Setting Your Church Free), as well as workshops on Getting Anger Under Control and Freedom from Fear.

He is co-presenter with Steve Goss in "The Grace Course." He lives with his wife, Shirley, in the mountains of western North Carolina. They have four young adult children.

40 DAYS OF GRACE

DISCOVERING GOD'S LIBERATING LOVE

RICH MILLER

MONARCH
BOOKS
Oxford, UK & Grand Rapids, Michigan, USA

Published by Monarch Books
an imprint of
Lion Hudson plc
Wilkinson House, Jordan Hill Road,
Oxford OX2 8DR, England
Email: monarch@lionhudson.com
www.lionhudson.com/monarch

ISBN 978 0 85721 443 0
e-ISBN 978 0 85721 458 4

First edition 2013

Acknowledgments
Unless otherwise stated, Scripture taken from the New American Standard Bible®, Copyright © 1960, 1962, 1963, 1968, 1971, 1972, 1973, 1975, 1977, 1995 by The Lockman Foundation. Used by permission. Scripture quotations marked NLT are taken from the Holy Bible, New Living Translation, copyright © 1996, 2004, 2007 by Tyndale House Foundation. Used by permission of Tyndale House Publishers, Inc., Carol Stream, Illinois 60188. All rights reserved.

Extract pages 89–90 copyright © 1988 Kevin Miller. Used with permission.

Every effort has been made to trace the original copyright holders where required. In some cases this has proved impossible. We shall be happy to correct any such omissions in future editions.

A catalogue record for this book is available from the British Library.

Printed and bound in the UK, June 2013, LH26

Dedication

I gratefully dedicate this book to my Mom, who was whisked away into the arms of Life Himself while the writing of this book was being finalized. She showed me grace when I needed it the most and appreciated it the least.

I also dedicate this book to my Dad, who is in the Truth, and who, when I was young, was convinced I would be a writer long before I ever held that dream.

You both did a great job of parenting, considering the raw material you had to work with. I'm referring to my older brother, of course...

Contents

Acknowledgments

When it came to writing this book (an honor that was certainly not deserved), I drew from my own resources in God, but also there is much in here that I could not have come up with on my own but was desperately needed. Much grace was certainly required to write a book on grace, and a huge chunk of that grace came through others.

First, thanks to Neil Anderson who got me started on writing books for Freedom in Christ Ministries back in the early 1990s. His life's work in Christ filled in a lot of missing pieces for me and gave me something worth writing about. Thanks, Neil, for helping me breathe fresher air and walk on more solid ground.

Second, kudos to my colleague Paul Travis who courageously bared his heart and soul in the book *Breaking the Bondage of Legalism*, which became the birthplace of The Grace Course and eventually this book. Go for it, Paul, in finishing up your next book!

Third, I want to say a big "thank you!" to my close friend and brother, Steve Goss. His invitation to bring me in on The Grace Course project was characteristic of his selfless life and style of ministry. The world is a freer place because of you, brother… even though your jokes are still awful.

Fourth, this is my first book with Monarch Books and I hope it's not the last. Tony Collins… we've come quite a way since sharing a couple of lemonades outside of a boiling hot church in late May, 2012. Your personal touch to this writing project has made it fun. Our new friendship is one of those surprise "grace gifts" God delights in plopping into our lives. Thanks, Tony, and to all the staff at Monarch for your hard work on this project. God's grace is sufficient.

Finally, I want to let my family... Shirley, Michelle, Brian, Emily, and Joshua Luke... know that God's gift of you energizes me far more than you'll ever know. May each of you truly be strong in the grace that is in Christ Jesus. There's no other way to fly!

Introduction

The fact that you are reading this means you are alive. Profound, huh? Well, that actually is a meaningful comment in the sense that being alive means you still have time to change. I still have time to change.

Do we *need* to change? That question should be a no-brainer unless you think you are God's gift to the world or something. But if you aren't sure if you are due for some change, just ask your spouse or your kids or your best friend. That should set you straight.

Are we *willing* to change? Ah… that is the tougher question to answer. It reminds me of a story told by eighteenth-century Danish religious philosopher, Søren Kierkegaard:

> There was a town where only ducks live. Every Sunday the ducks would waddle out of their houses and waddle down Main Street to their church. They waddled into the sanctuary and squatted in their proper pews. The duck choir waddled in and took its place, then the duck minister would come forward and open the duck Bible. He would read to them, "Ducks! God has given you wings! With wings you can fly! With wings you can mount up and soar like eagles. No walls can confine you! No fence can hold you! You have wings. God has given you wings and you can fly like birds." All the ducks shouted "AMEN!"… and they all waddled home.[1]

That story is funny because it is so real, so typical of how we are. Being told what we should do, even by a great preacher, doesn't mean we'll do it. We have to want to and see our need to change. And let's face it. Most of us, if we are honest, don't like to change. Even if what we are doing is flawed, at least it is familiar. It is kind of scary and seems like a lot of work to give up what we are used to doing, though we may be painfully aware that it is not working very well.

Maybe how you are relating to God isn't working particularly well.

There are two fundamentally different approaches to living life in relation to God... aside, of course, from simply trying to ignore Him and live as if He doesn't exist. That strategy, by the way, is not recommended.

The first approach is to jump up and down, trying to impress God with who you are and what you can do, hoping He will pick you for His team or keep you on the team, so to speak.

The second is to relate to Him on the basis of grace.

Though the first approach makes sense at first glance (since it is the way we get noticed in this world), it comes with a whole load of baggage. If we are going to change from this way of relating to God, we need to face some of the heavier burdens that way of living generates – namely guilt, shame, fear and pride –and discover the way out. We'll do that in the pages ahead.

The way of grace is much more subtle but is the way that God actually has chosen to work. We'll finish off this book looking at how to live in grace rather than in *dis*grace, and you'll have the chance to choose, the chance to change. In other words, you can waddle or you can fly.

One of Jesus' followers, John, wrote:

For the Law was given through Moses; grace and truth were realized through Jesus Christ.

John 1:17

Grace and truth – despite what some might think – are not opponents; they are friends. Grace is like the clean, oxygen-rich atmosphere we breathe. It is necessary for life, for health, for growth. When you are surrounded by grace you flourish; when you're not, you gasp for air. You feel like you are being smothered. Graceless living is like choking pollutants in the air – or worse, like carbon monoxide. You may not even realize it is killing you spiritually until it is too late.

Truth, on the other hand, is the solid ground on which we stand, move and live. It is spiritual terra firma. When truth is not around, you stumble and trip over hidden obstacles. You fall into potholes and pits, turning your ankle, breaking your leg, making it impossible to stand or walk. In the severest absence of truth, your path becomes a trap of spiritual quicksand that will ensnare you and suffocate you unless you find true help.

We need both grace and truth in order to live. In other words, we need Jesus. Are you willing to let Jesus show you how to live rather than muddling along in the way that naturally seems best to you? In other words, are you willing to change?

But I'm getting ahead of myself. I'll leave the walking to you and let you draw your own conclusions during these *40 Days of Grace*. In these pages I have tried to teach the truth about grace so that this forty-day journey – whichever path you ultimately choose to take – will be a brisk one on a firm path with tons of fresh air to enjoy.

You will find quite a few forks in the road as you travel. The best path to take is not always easy, but it is wise. And I believe it is clear, though it is the road less traveled. It is the path of grace.

Amazing Grace

Day 1: Let Me Introduce You to Grace!

I got married when I was thirty-five years old, back in 1989. My wife's name is Shirley Grace and I'm really glad I married her, because God knew I surely needed a lot of grace!

I remember the first time I met her. It was actually ten years before we got married, in 1979. She was sitting by a swimming pool in Myrtle Beach, South Carolina. I was twenty-five years old and a dashing young man. She was (and is!) gorgeous. That was the first thing I noticed about her! Soon after, of course, I came to know and appreciate her cheerful disposition, her gentle, nurturing spirit and her zealous heart for Jesus as well.

Now, you might be wondering, "If she was so amazing, inside and out, why did it take you so long to get around to marrying her?" Great question!

There were a lot of reasons: the busyness of life, not living anywhere near each other, my need to grow up in some ways... that sort of thing. But the main reason was that I was used to living on my own and the idea of being married was kind of scary. Decades later, I can't imagine living without her, but back then I had no idea how good it would be.

God offers us a new life of grace and yet so many of God's people still seem to live life as independent, "single" people. Why is that? If God's grace is so amazing, inside and out, why does it take so many of us so long to get around to living by and in grace? Great question!

This might be a really good time to let me introduce you to grace! Maybe you have "met" before, but through the busyness of life, not hanging around much together, and your need to grow up in some ways, you and grace have kind of fallen on hard times. Maybe the thought of living by God's grace rather than independently, by your own resources, seems... well... kind of scary.

Romans 5:1–2 says:

> Therefore, having been justified by faith, we have peace with God through our Lord Jesus Christ, through whom also we have obtained our introduction by faith into this grace in which we stand; and we exult in hope of the glory of God.

We'll talk more next week about being justified (made not guilty) by faith, so hang in there on that part. But just as we are introduced to and enter into a life of freedom from guilt by faith, so we also obtain our introduction into God's grace by faith.

You might be familiar with Ephesians 2:8–9:

> For by grace you have been saved through faith; and that not of yourselves, it is the gift of God; not as a result of works, so that no one may boast.

It might be helpful to translate this verse into a mathematical-type equation. All right, I admit to being left-brained, so all you right-brainers just humor me for a moment, OK?

> God's grace + Our faith in Jesus = Being saved or rescued from sin and its penalty

The idea in Ephesians 2 of our rescue from sin being a gift of

God is very important. That's really what grace is: a free gift that we don't deserve. Some define it as "unmerited favor." In short, grace is God freely giving us what we don't deserve and can't come up with on our own, but what we desperately need.

Pretty amazing, isn't it?

We obtain our introduction into God's grace when we, by faith, receive God's free gift of forgiveness in Christ. We turn away from our self-centered, independent lifestyle (the Bible calls this sin), and realize His death on the cross was full payment for our sins. In response, we open our hearts to Jesus to forgive us and take charge of our lives, believing that He rose from the dead and is now very much alive!

Like any gift, however, God's grace must be received, but unlike a Christmas present or birthday gift, which we can see, God's gift of forgiveness (His grace) is not visible. Therefore it must be received, not by sight, but by faith. By "faith" I mean that we believe God is telling us the truth and that He is who He says He is and will do what He says He'll do, and we say "yes" to Him. We believe. That's faith.

Have you ever received this free gift from God? If so, you have already been introduced to grace! If you haven't, we encourage you to do so as soon as your heart is open.

For those who have already been introduced to grace, how is your "relationship" with grace going? It's remarkable to me that many who started out so well, being so excited about and grateful for God's saving, rescuing grace, somehow take a wrong turn away from grace at some point. Most probably they don't even realize they've gotten off track.

It's kind of like we gradually get tricked into believing that somewhere along the race of life God changed the rules. We start off well, trusting in God alone to supply what we need and to enable us to live life, but then down the road we come to believe it is "up to us" to make the Christian life work.

The apostle Paul couldn't figure out how and why some of his friends had made that wrong turn away from grace and faith. He wrote:

> This is the only thing I want to find out from you: did you receive the Spirit by the works of the Law, or by hearing with faith? Are you so foolish? Having begun by the Spirit, are you now being perfected by the flesh [your own human effort]?
>
> Galatians 3:2

The way it works is simple. You come to Jesus and receive His free gift (grace) of rescue from sin's penalty by faith. And God gives you the Holy Spirit at that moment... by faith. Then you grow in Christ the same way. God gives you all you need in love, power and wisdom as a gift of grace, and you walk (live) in His provision... by faith. Paul writes elsewhere:

> Therefore as you have received Christ Jesus the Lord, so walk in Him...
>
> Colossians 2:6

How did you receive Christ Jesus the Lord? By grace through faith. So how do you walk (live life) in Christ? By grace through faith. God provides what we need (which includes a community of faith, called the Church), and we live our lives fully dependent on His provision. Like I said, it's simple. Why do we so often make it complex?

Maybe this really is your introduction to grace. Or maybe you are just beginning to get reacquainted, rekindling an old flame, so to speak. Either way, welcome.

I've been married for a couple decades. I've been in Christ, living by faith in His grace, much longer. In both cases, I can't imagine living any other way.

A THOUGHT TO CHEW ON

Living by grace doesn't end when you come to Christ; that's just the beginning!

A TRUTH TO REMEMBER

"Through [Christ] we have obtained our introduction by faith into this grace in which we stand..." (Romans 5:2).

A QUESTION TO MULL OVER

How would you describe your relationship with grace? Strangers? Polite acquaintances? Close friends? Falling in love? What relationship? Something else?

TALKING IT OVER WITH GOD

Father, it's really easy to fall back into thinking that this life is pretty much up to me. After all, almost from the time I was born, the whole world system is designed for me to learn to live life on my own... to not be dependent on anyone... to be "grown up," which translates into becoming increasingly self-reliant and self-sufficient. I know that there's no way I can save myself and so in that way it's kind of easy to see how much I need You. But isn't it a sign of weakness to have to live by faith in Your grace every moment of every day? I guess I have to admit that my relationship with grace needs some work.

I really hope You can be patient with me as I learn to walk by this grace in which I now stand. Are you gracious enough to not get mad at me even though I start out at a crawl? The Bible says You are kind and patient and all that, but sometimes I doubt. Thanks for listening. Amen.

Day 2: Is God Gracious?

"To be honest with you, I haven't thought about God very much lately."

That was the honest admission of the lady sitting in the aisle seat as I was flying out of Atlanta. I was by the window, thankful for the extra elbow room the vacant middle seat afforded. I had let her know that my job was to basically help people get "unstuck" and experience the most life has to offer by getting to know God. I could tell she was curious though skeptical.

"My grandmother forced religion on all of us, and nobody had the backbone to refuse her," she continued. "That was probably smart, since I think she could have whipped us all!" She smiled as she retold the stories of her grandmother's amazing cooking exploits, serving up world-class meals for their entire clan. I could almost smell the lasagna!

It was clear that this woman's grandmother, though a great cook, was the strict matriarch of the family, and what she wanted, she got. So the whole family would dutifully trudge off to church on Sundays, and for weddings, funerals, baptisms and holidays. Fed up with church, God and anything to do with religion, Valerie (not her real name) had fled from her family's stifling religious tradition as soon as she grew up.

When the smoke cleared and the dust settled from the stories of her life, Valerie had come to one very clear conclusion: If God had anything to do with her grandmother's stuffy, straitjacket religion, she wanted nothing to do with Him.

And I had to agree. I wouldn't want anything to do with an ultra-religious, punishing God like that either. But in the next breath, I assured her He wasn't like that at all.

When she looked at me, I don't think I was mistaken when I thought I saw something different on her face. I think it was *hope*.

Sensing that she probably knew very little about the Bible, I just started telling stories from the gospels. I told her about how Jesus loved to heal people on the Sabbath day and how that drove the religious people crazy because they had put God in a box. They thought they had God all figured out and their box did not include any kind of work, by God or anyone else, on Saturday (the Sabbath). I guess Jesus never got that memo!

I related the story of how a woman caught in adultery had been dragged to Jesus and how the men of that town challenged the Lord with the Jewish legal requirement that she be stoned. And then all the men walked away, dropping their stones and dropping the charges against the woman because Jesus challenged the one who was without sin to hurl the first rock. Pretty shrewd. You see, the Law required at least two witnesses and when Jesus was the only one left, there was no longer any legal "quorum" to condemn her. Instead, Jesus gave her a new lease on life, a second chance to live the right way… which was His plan all along.

Valerie was drinking it all in like thirsty ground. Her face was sending two messages: "Could God *really* be like this?" and "Tell me more!"

So I did.

I was almost in tears as I told her about our Lord cleansing the lowliest of the low of that day, the lepers… touching them when others were running for their lives the other way for fear of catching their disease. Then came the story of the sinful woman who anointed Jesus with expensive perfume and whom Jesus sent away in peace due to her faith. And on and on I shared with a passion that could only have come from the Spirit of the Lord.

"I've never heard these things before," she said, shaking her head. "This is so different a picture of God than I was taught."

As we were preparing for landing I turned to Valerie and said, "I think it's time that you come to know God as He really is rather than how you've been taught."

"I think I'd like that," she concluded, nodding her head.

I wonder how many people are like this woman. They have been fed a pack of religious lies about who God is and have, understandably, exited stage left from the Church.

Some people have read or heard bits and pieces of the Old Testament and have formed a picture of God as an angry, wrathful, punishing God. Then they hear stories about Jesus that seem to indicate that He's a lot different than that – kind, merciful and caring. And so they are confused. They cringe in fear of the Old Testament God while hoping for clemency from the New Testament Jesus. As a result, many experience religion as an attempt to avoid or appease an angry Father, while hoping that the meek and mild Jesus will take up their cause and help them get into heaven somehow.

What a religious mess!

It is interesting to note that when Moses got really close to the Old Testament God and asked to see His glory, the Lord Himself made all His goodness pass before him. Since God's glory is too much for a mere mortal to handle, God protected Moses and then let him see His back. As the Lord passed by, God described Himself. And this is what He said in Exodus 34:6–7:

> The LORD, the LORD God, compassionate and gracious, slow to anger, and abounding in lovingkindness and truth; who keeps lovingkindness for thousands, who forgives iniquity, transgression and sin; yet He will by no means leave the guilty unpunished…

The way a lot of people would describe God, it would sound more like:

The LORD, the LORD God, mad as hell and angry as a
hornet. If you watch your step and keep your nose
clean, you might just make it. But I wouldn't count on it
because the LORD knows how much you screw up...

How did God identify Himself in His own words to Moses?
Compassionate. Gracious. Slow to anger. Abounding in
lovingkindness and truth. Forgiving. And yes, He will
punish those who are guilty and who reject Him, but would
you really have respect for a God who was soft and wishy-
washy on sin and who would let the human race get away
with murder?

A number of times in the Psalms, God is identified in
similar terms to how He revealed Himself to Moses. Psalm
145:8–9 is one of them:

The LORD is gracious and merciful;
Slow to anger and great in lovingkindness.
The LORD is good to all,
And His mercies are over all His works.

So what about Jesus? Is He somehow different than the God of
the Old Testament? Actually – though it's a surprise to many –
they are exactly the same. In John 14:9 Jesus said to Philip:

He who has seen Me has seen the Father.

So there you are. Jesus is like the Father and the Father is like
Jesus. They are identical in nature. And God, by the way, never
changes (Malachi 3:6) and neither does Jesus (Hebrews 13:8).
Therefore we can conclude that in nature and character the
God of the Old Testament is the same as the God of the New
Testament, and God the Father is the same as God the Son, the
Lord Jesus Christ. And God is gracious and merciful.

And if Valerie seeks Him, she will find Him. And she will be filled with joy. And so will you, because He is gracious.

A THOUGHT TO CHEW ON

God the Father and Jesus Christ have the same nature and they are gracious and merciful.

A TRUTH TO REMEMBER

"He who has seen Me has seen the Father" (Jesus' words in John 14:9).

A QUESTION TO MULL OVER

Do you see God as Someone to run to because He is gracious and merciful or are you afraid that He is angry, frustrated or disgusted with you?

TALKING IT OVER WITH GOD

Dear Father, I wonder if You realize how hard it is to talk to Somebody that I can't see or hear. Forgive me if the words of my prayers don't make a whole lot of sense to You. I guess I'll learn how to pray better the more I practice.

Anyway, I've got to admit that some of the stories in the Bible are pretty scary. After all, You did have a habit in the Old Testament of wiping out large numbers of people. True, they were pretty wicked, but it makes me afraid that You might see me like them and then it would be all over. And yet the Bible says that You are gracious and merciful.

It's a little bit hard to wrap my mind around all that, but I want to. And I can see that Jesus is really patient and kind. But to realize that You and Jesus are the same and that You are, therefore, patient and kind, too, and that You really care about me, well... that's pretty mind-blowing.

But I guess it shouldn't surprise me that there are things about You that I can't quite get, since You are God and I'm not. Help me to see that as a good thing. Thanks again for listening. Amen.

Day 3: The Father Wound

Author John Eldredge popularized the term "the father wound" to describe the deep, core damage done by dads who abuse, neglect, or desert their children, or are otherwise just not around or involved in healthy ways with them. The result? A whole Pandora's box of pain, suffering and harmful "acting out" in the lives of those kids... as well as the cycle of father wounding likely being passed down to the next generation, and the next... apart from the grace of God.

The other day I was chatting with one of my son Brian's friends about his family background. William (not his real name) had lived in Los Angeles early in his life, but at the age of three his parents had divorced and his mom had moved back east to North Carolina with him. She eventually remarried, as did his dad, and so William has a set of half-brothers and half-sisters on both coasts. Most of his extended family still lives out in LA and he was a bit sad that this was the first year that he wouldn't be traveling out there to see them all. He usually did that for about three weeks each summer.

"When you go out there, do you stay with your dad?" I asked William.

"I usually stay different places," he replied, not looking me in the eye.

"Your relationship with your dad... is it a close one?" I probed.

Shaking his head, the nineteen-year-old quietly responded, "My dad... he's pretty much never been there for me."

The father wound.

I had just finished doing a youth conference at which I had spoken about the critical need to forgive those who have hurt us. When I do these events, I don't engage in parent-bashing in general or dad-bashing in particular. Not at all. After all, I am a parent and a dad myself. And it's really hard work. But the reality of life is that those closest to us have the greatest capacity to wound us most deeply, because we are counting on them to love us and provide for us and protect us. And since parents are the primary givers of those things when we are children, parents also have the greatest potential for doing harm during those crucial, formative years.

After the teaching portion of the conference was over, there was a time for people to talk about what God had done in their lives during the event. A young man about sixteen years old got up and told his story of abuse and neglect in his home. The crowd of 150 or so teenagers was all ears.

"Every day during the past eight years, my dad told me that he wished I'd never been born, that I was a mistake."

The father wound.

A number of years ago in Mexico I was speaking at an event for Christian workers and their families. Since this was such a strategic group of men and women, I made sure to carve out time to meet individually with some folks needing personal attention. One of them was a young lady in her twenties. It turned out that her dad (who had died prior to our meeting) was at one time the head of a major Christian organization in that nation.

Knowing her dad was not there to defend himself, I tried to be objective as his daughter described him.

"He was always gone and never had time for me. When he would finally come home, he yelled at my mom, he yelled at me. He was too tired out or busy or preoccupied to do things with the family. It seemed like the ministry was much more important to him than we were.

"I grew to hate him. Even though he's dead, I still hate him."

Not surprisingly, this young lady had come to believe that her heavenly Father was basically the same as her earthly dad. She had very little interest in God.

The father wound.

In the parable of the prodigal son found in Luke 15, Jesus told a story about two young men and their dad. The older son, like so many first-borns, was conscientious, hard-working and dutiful. The younger son, like so many second-borns, was the exact opposite. He basically wanted to party! So he took his share of the inheritance and went wild... until the money ran out, and he had to hire himself out to feed pigs. One day he came to his senses and decided it would be a lot smarter to go back home and become a hired hand than to wallow in the muck and mire he had made of life on his own. So he rehearsed the lines of apology he would tell his dad and... let's pick up the story from Luke 15:20:

> So he got up and came to his father. But while he was still a long way off, his father saw him and felt compassion for him, and ran and embraced him and kissed him.

It might surprise you to know that the reason Jesus told this story was to show us how God the Father responds to us when we go our own way, mess up our lives and then come back to Him. The father in the story is a picture of God the Father. And just from this short story from Jesus, we can tell at least three things about God.

First, *God gives us freedom to fail*. Though it was culturally very wrong for the younger son to demand his inheritance prior to this father's death, his dad gave it to him anyway. And he let the young man go. He could have controlled him and forced him to remain home. But he didn't. That shows God's respect for our dignity as human beings He has created in His image with the capacity to choose to do good… or not.

Second, *God never gives up waiting for our return*. The father in the story spotted his kid while he was still a long way off. That means he was looking for him and had never given up hope that he would one day return. And so God is with us. He is always watching, looking down the road, longing for our return to Him. But He patiently waits until we come to our senses and come home of our own volition.

Third, *God's heart is so big it nearly bursts with joy when we come back to Him*. The father in the story was filled with compassion and couldn't wait for his son to come all the way back. He ran to meet him (something very culturally uncool in Jesus' day), hugged him and kissed him.

Can you picture God this way?

Jesus wasn't just telling nice stories to give people warm fuzzies so they'd give Him money or something. Jesus was telling the truth. He wanted us to know just how crazy in love with us God the Father is.

No Father wound.

After a message I gave on forgiving from the heart, a young man came up to me and asked if I would talk with his friend Jonathan (not his real name).

When I walked over to where Jonathan was seated, he was sobbing so hard that we couldn't understand a word he was trying to say. We just had to sit back and wait for him to calm down. Eventually we figured out that he had been deeply hurt by his dad cutting him down. He was also very upset that his dad had committed adultery.

After a bit of encouragement, Jonathan was able to let go of the anger and hatred he felt and sincerely forgave his dad for those things. But God had done something supernatural to bring Jonathan to that point. He came up to me three days later and told me.

In that message on forgiveness, I had used the same story of the prodigal son that I wrote about in today's devotional. That didn't sit well with Jonathan.

"I have hated that parable," he confessed, "because everybody uses it and I've heard it so much!"

Wanting to get out of the meeting as quickly as possible, however, so he wouldn't have to listen to that hated parable, Jonathan encountered a problem he hadn't expected.

"I couldn't get out of my seat!" he shouted, eyes bulging. I could just imagine an angel with a finger resting on Jonathan's head saying, "Not so fast, Buster!"

Father wound healed.

The younger son in the Luke 15 story knew he could come back home to his dad because he knew his dad was full of grace. Do you know that you, too, can come back to your heavenly Father because He is full of grace? Romans 2:4 says:

> Or do you think lightly of the riches of His kindness and tolerance and patience, not knowing that the kindness of God leads you to repentance?

Who would ever want to come back to an angry and condemning God? Nobody. But when we realize that God is kind, patient, gracious and merciful, there's no holding us back from coming home to Him!

God is the Father you have always needed and wanted. And you can come home today.

A THOUGHT TO CHEW ON

God's heart and arms are always open to you. Only the Father can heal the father wound.

A TRUTH TO REMEMBER

"The kindness of God leads you to repentance" (Romans 2:4).

A QUESTION TO MULL OVER

Where might you find yourself in the Luke 15 story? Eager to get out on your own to party? Living it up, living wild? Running out of time and running out of money? Stuck in some dead-end life knowing your own foolishness got you there? Coming to your senses? Coming home?

TALKING IT OVER WITH GOD

Dear Father, it's pretty amazing to me that You, the God who created the whole universe and holds it all together effortlessly, would be described by Your Son as a Dad who watches for His kid, races out to meet him and hugs and kisses him even though he is dirty, smelly, broken and bad. I guess that's why they call it amazing grace. This really changes the game. It takes faith out of the realm of sterile religion and puts it onto the muddy playing field of real life.

I have to admit that there's been pain in my life – some of it caused by others and some of it brought on by my own stupid decisions. But I guess You know all that already. Maybe I'm starting to come to my senses. At least it feels like that might be happening. It's good to know that when I come home, You'll be the first One to meet me. Amen.

Day 4: A Celebrating God

I don't know about you, but it's hard for me sometimes to picture God really cutting loose, laughing, joking around, celebrating, dancing and being the life of the party. Somehow it seems a bit undignified for the God of the universe to act that way. It's kind of like how I'd probably feel if my ninety-year-old dad decided to frequent the local bars and hang out with the twenty-something blondes. I mean, it just somehow wouldn't seem right, though some people would find it amusing or even cute, I suppose. But I doubt they (or I) would respect him for doing that. By the way, my dad doesn't do that kind of thing, much to my relief!

Maybe I've seen too many of those insipid paintings of Jesus where He is depicted as this emaciated, blond, stringy-haired white guy holding a lamb and doing that weird sort of peace sign or *Star Wars* thing with His hand. It's hard to imagine a guy really having a good time while he's carrying around a lamb, for heaven's sake. Plus that halo around His head… Seeing that come into the room would kill a party pretty quick, I would think.

If you have been of the same opinion that I have, prepare to have your world rocked. Because God really is a celebrating God! If you think I'm crazy, then go back with me to the story of the father and the two sons in Luke 15. Let's pick it up from right after the father races out to meet the kid, hugs him and kisses him (and that scene should have tipped you off that God is not sad, sour, strait-laced and somber!):

> And the son said to him, "Father, I have sinned against
> heaven, and in your sight; I am no longer worthy to
> be called your son." But the father said to his slaves,
> "Quickly bring out the best robe and put it on him, and

put a ring on his hand and sandals on his feet; and bring
the fattened calf, kill it, and let us eat and celebrate; for
this son of mine was dead and has come to life again;
he was lost and has been found." And they began to
celebrate.

Luke 15:21–24

Remember that Jesus told this story so that the stuffy religious leaders of the day could see how God the Father responds to His children who come back home to Him. And the text is clear: He celebrates!

As I read this section of Luke 15, a couple of things stand out to me.

First, the son made his speech and delivered his lines of apology flawlessly, but it's almost like the father wasn't even listening. Let's be honest, if you or I had a kid that had just taken all our hard-earned inheritance and blown it on booze and floozies, don't you think we'd have wanted to have a bit of a talk with the lad? Isn't it perhaps just a bit possible that we might be a tad angry with the boy? But there isn't even a trace of any of that with the father. He is just so overjoyed that his son has come home that he turns into Dad the Party Planner. Throwing a party for a boy who could easily, and truthfully, be described as a self-centered, irresponsible, entitled brat is about the last thing in the world most people would do. But that's exactly what the father (symbolizing God the Father) did!

Second, the generosity of the father is astounding. He has the best robe in the house put on the kid (the boy's clothes were likely pretty ratty). He has the ring of the father's authority put on his son's finger. And then he has his bare feet sandaled, which was an honor enjoyed only by the father and his sons. In other words, the boy was immediately, completely and unconditionally restored to his place of sonship. The boy thought himself unworthy to be a son; he was willing to work as a hired hand. The father had no such thoughts. Notice he referred to him as "this son of mine." There was no shame, no disrespect, no probation period to see if he was really repentant.

Third, the father entered into the celebration – no doubt with unbridled exuberance. Why? Because his son was dead and had come back to life; he was lost but now was found. Sound familiar? You're right. "I once was lost but now am found" is one of the lines from the hymn "Amazing Grace."

Yes, the father – who, I repeat, is symbolic of our heavenly Father – not only threw a party but celebrated at the party!

Now, it's instructive to note the reason for the party. It wasn't some Animal House orgy or a celebration just as an excuse to get drunk or high. God would never be a party to such a party. When God celebrates, He has a legitimate reason. And that's the case in the story Jesus told. The father's son had repented and come back home. That is *really* a reason to throw a party! And celebration in heaven for such a reason seems to be the rule rather than the exception (perish all thoughts that heaven will be boring!). Look at Luke 15:8–10, another story that Jesus told:

> Or what woman, if she has ten silver coins and loses one coin, does not light a lamp and sweep the house and search carefully until she finds it? When she has found it, she calls together her friends and neighbors, saying, "Rejoice with me, for I have found the coin which I had lost!" In the same way, I tell you, there is joy in the presence of the angels of God over one sinner who repents.

Apparently Jesus was truly free to have a good time, but it was always for a legitimate reason – celebrating God and His wonderful work on earth. Jesus turned water into wine at a wedding feast when the first batch of wine ran out. Jesus had been invited to that wedding, by the way, and party poopers don't get invited to such things! You can read all about it in John 2:1–12.

Jesus had no qualms about eating and drinking with so-called sinners. In fact, the Pharisees really had their noses out of joint from Jesus' habits. Jesus recounted their accusations of Him in Matthew 11:19 when He said:

> The Son of Man came eating and drinking, and they say, "Behold, a gluttonous man and a drunkard, a friend of tax collectors and sinners!"

Of course, their assessments of Jesus as a glutton and drunk were wrong, but you don't get called such things by being squeamish around earthy people having a good time. Jesus clearly enjoyed life and celebrated exuberantly over the right things.

Now, what's the point of all this? Basically one thing. One of Satan's most prevalent slanders against the character of God is that He is a cosmic killjoy. Kind of like, "Hey, if you want to lose all the fun in life and become one of those dull, boring Christians, go ahead." And everybody said, "No thanks!"

I hope you see that God is not like that at all. God has fun – for all the right reasons. And if you want all heaven to party, just come back home.

A THOUGHT TO CHEW ON

All heaven celebrates when someone comes back home to the Father.

A TRUTH TO REMEMBER

"'Let us eat and celebrate; for this son of mine was dead and has come to life again; he was lost and has been found.' And they began to celebrate" (Luke 15:23–24).

A QUESTION TO MULL OVER

How are you responding to the idea of a celebrating God? Does it make you angry? Do you think it demeans Him? Does it bring a smile to your face? Does it encourage you to want to draw closer to Him? Does it soften your heart to want to come back to Him?

TALKING IT OVER WITH GOD

Dear Father, I'm not sure what to do with today's reading. I know that You are pure and perfect and that You can't even be tempted to sin… let alone sin. I guess I always had this picture of You that You were somehow "above" things like fun, celebrating and even partying. But You created joy and pleasure and laughter and celebration, so why would You not fully and freely enter into it in such a way that in no way sullies Your character, but in reality shines the light even brighter on Your goodness and greatness?

The whole point of this is to break down any walls that have kept me from seeking You and walking through life with You. And knowing that You delight in me and are thrilled to the point of exuberant celebration when I come back to You… well, that knocks down a huge wall.

Thanks for being Yourself. You and Your grace truly are amazing. Amen.

Day 5: There's Another Brother

I have a godly friend and colleague in ministry. His name is Paul Travis and he and I have spent many hours in prayer together. Paul is in the latter years of his life and ministry but his heart still burns with a zeal for seeing God's people walk in the newness, freshness and grace of life that is ours in Christ. Paul is such an avid student of the Bible that he probably has enough notes to write a library full of books. I had the honor of collaborating on the writing of one with him a few years back. Here is an autobiographical excerpt about Paul's life from that book:

> I had always performed well. Though I would likely
> have denied it vehemently, I was a legalist, a spiritual
> performer. Driven to work hard for God, I had already
> accomplished many things in my ministry. If there had
> been an Academy Award for "best performance" by
> a leading actor in church, I would have been up there
> receiving the Oscar. In fact, I would have received the
> "Lifetime Performance Award" because from the womb
> to the tomb I was bound and determined to do right,
> look right, and be right. It was only then that I believed I
> would be all right. But I was wrong.[2]

I really appreciate Paul's candid assessment of his life. Dr Neil Anderson lovingly refers to Paul as "a recovering fundamentalist." And Paul has genuinely shifted the foundation of his life radically from works to grace, though he'd be the first one to admit that old habits die hard.

How can such a conscientious, hard-working lifestyle be *wrong*? Let's go back to Jesus' teaching in Luke 15 and see if we can find an answer to that question:

Now his older son was in the field, and when he came and approached the house, he heard music and dancing. And he summoned one of the servants and began inquiring what these things could be. And he said to him, "Your brother has come, and your father has killed the fattened calf because he has received him back safe and sound." But he became angry and was not willing to go in; and his father came out and began pleading with him. But he answered and said to his father, "Look! For so many years I have been serving you and I have never neglected a command of yours; and yet you have never given me a young goat, so that I might celebrate with my friends; but when this son of yours came, who has devoured your wealth with prostitutes, you killed the fattened calf for him." And he said to him, "Son, you have always been with me, and all that is mine is yours. But we had to celebrate and rejoice, for this brother of yours was dead and has begun to live, and was lost and has been found."

Luke 15:25–32

And that's how the story ends. Jesus stops right there. Even though the saga of the younger son has a happy ending, Jesus leaves (intentionally, we can assume) the final chapter of the older son's life open-ended. The story doesn't end with an exclamation point. It ends with a question mark. Does the older son's heart soften toward his brother and his dad? Does he join the party? Or does he angrily pick up his shovel and go back to work, shaking his head at all the injustice in the world? We don't know.

There are several things about the older son's beliefs and behavior that Jesus teaches in this story.

First, the older son held in a lot of resentment toward his dad. The word he used for "serving" means "slaving away." He worked hard, no doubt about it. But it was joyless work. Kind of how my kids feel about the work they do at a local fast-food restaurant: They like the money and need the money, but they can't stand the work. (It does provide them with a strong motivation to get a college education, though!) The older son was responsible and faithful in what he did. That is, his behavior outwardly was right. But he viewed his dad as being a totally unfair taskmaster. He had a lot of time out in the fields to formulate his opinion of his father, and his inner attitude had become bitter and his reason for serving was all wrong.

Is it any surprise to you to know that God is not only concerned about *what* we do, but also *why* we do it?

Second, the older son was totally unaware of all he was and all he had as a son. The father said, "you have always been with me." Can you see the affection the father had for his boy? But it was totally lost on the kid. The father saw him as a beloved son. The son felt like a slave. The father also said, "all that is mine is yours." The older son could have had a goat or a calf or a whole flock of goats or a whole herd of cows if he'd simply asked for it. But he never did. The older son was living as a slave, not as a son. He existed in poverty when he could have been living life to the full.

It is very possible to be in a working, slaving, servant–Master relationship with God and totally miss the joy of being a child of our heavenly Father and miss out on all the gifts of His grace that come with that privilege.

Third, the older son held in a lot of resentment toward his younger brother. He had basically disowned him. Notice he refers to his sibling in his argument with his dad as "this son of yours." The father tries to remind him of the relationship, correcting him by referring to the younger son as "this brother of yours."

God is always "into" relationships – first in connecting us in a love–trust relationship with Himself, and second in leading us into healthy friendships with others.

Take the four pictures of the boys. The first picture is of the younger son living wildly in the world. The second picture is of the sorry, apologetic, broken kid shuffling home. The third picture is of the young son embraced by the father, restored to his place in the family, celebrating his new life. The fourth picture is of the older brother, faithfully slaving away, "righteously indignant" over the sinful condition of others.

Sadly, too often we find ourselves resembling the son in the first or second picture. Or we mistakenly applaud or reward those who are in the fourth.

My prayer is that we discover the joy of the third picture and find ourselves drawn to that place of rest and joy in the Father. I know that's where I want to be. How about you?

A THOUGHT TO CHEW ON

It is possible to do all the "right things" for all the wrong reasons.

A TRUTH TO REMEMBER

"Son, you have always been with me, and all that is mine is yours" (Luke 15:31).

A QUESTION TO MULL OVER

Which picture of the two sons best describes where you are right now in your life? What needs to change in order for you to embrace the third picture as truly portraying your life?

TALKING IT OVER WITH GOD

Dear Father, please take a good look at my heart and tell me what You see. When I think about those pictures of the sons, here's what I'd like to be true of me: I'd like to come to my senses and come home like the second picture. I'd then really like to receive all the good gifts of Your grace that You want to give me, celebrating my true place as Your dearly loved child, like the third picture. But I don't want to just sing and dance and feast for the rest of my life. I want to go on mission with You and serve with You in Your kingdom… not slaving away in resentment like the fourth picture, but joyfully obedient and walking with You in close friendship and a love–trust relationship with You. I guess that's a fifth picture not depicted in the story.

Now that You know what I'd like to be, please reveal to me where my heart is now in relationship with You, and do everything You need to and want to in order to make me all that You created me to be in Christ. I know the whole process won't be easy, so please give me the courage I need to stick with it. Amen.

Day 6: Grace Works

I could tell that our son, Brian, was struggling. He was sharing a room with his younger, adopted brother, Luke, and even though their bunk beds gave them some more space in the room, I could tell things were getting too close for comfort… at least for Brian.

We had adopted Luke from an orphanage in Thailand when he was four years old and though we can't imagine our family without him, he has presented some unique challenges. One of those challenges is that Luke, early on in life, had major boundary issues. He had no clue where his world was supposed to stop and somebody else's was to begin. Therefore, he became a pervasive, invasive presence with our other kids' stuff and they didn't know how to handle it.

Prior to adopting Luke, we had numerous foster children in our home and so our biological kids learned how to adjust to various problematic behaviors… at least, as well as little kids can! But Luke proved to be a particularly daunting challenge to them.

When the other three were playing a game, Luke would burst onto the scene and disrupt and often destroy what they were doing. After enduring this for a while, our kids decided on a strategy to protect themselves. They simply locked him out of their lives by locking him out of the room where they would play together.

Since kids coming out of orphanages typically have issues of rejection anyway, this pragmatic solution, though effective on one level, wasn't going to cut it. So I called the three together and had a straight talk with them.

"Kids, Luke is not a foster brother. We cannot take him back for someone else. Luke is your brother and is here to stay, and so you are going to have to find a way to open your hearts

– and your door – to him." With that, we prayed, and their "closed door policy" was abandoned. As they opened their door, they also opened their hearts. I was thrilled with their obedience.

Against the backdrop of that repentance, Brian was still really frustrated with Luke because his boundary issues persisted to the point where he was breaking a lot of Brian's stuff. The tops of most of his athletic trophies were broken off by Luke, for example.

Brian couldn't bring himself to spend any time with his brother. He disliked him, was frustrated that he had to room with him and avoided him as much as possible. I could've said something to him like: "Brian, I don't care what Luke has done. You need to spend time with him. Go up there and play with him now!"

Even though that was what eventually needed to happen, simply telling Brian what he should do might have resulted in outward obedience, for a while, but there would have been no change of heart. And remember, God is very concerned not only with *what* we do but also with *why* we do it.

This was a job for grace.

One of the difficulties with Luke is that he has a limited ability to understand what is being spoken to him and a very limited ability to verbally respond. He also tends to look away when you're talking with him. All these things made it likely that any attempt by Brian to directly address the issue with Luke would be unfruitful and probably very frustrating.

I had Brian sit in a chair and imagine Luke sitting on the edge of the lower bunk bed listening quietly and with understanding to everything his older brother said to him. Then I prayed and moved out of Brian's line of sight to see what would happen.

At first slowly, then with increased fluidity and intensity, Brian poured out his heart to Luke, expressing all his frustrations and telling Luke he wanted him to stop what he was doing. You would have sworn Luke was there.

After he got all his anger out, I encouraged Brian to express to Luke his forgiveness of him. He did so readily. I could tell Brian was really relieved.

What happened next floored me. Brian went directly upstairs and, of his own accord, went to Luke and played with him non-stop for forty-five minutes. He had *never* done that before.

Some people are under the mistaken impression that if you walk in grace and seek to help others walk in grace, no work will ever get done. They are afraid that people will take grace as an invitation to do nothing. I contend that if that occurs, then true grace is not in operation. Because grace works. Look at what Titus 2:11–14 says:

> For the grace of God has appeared, bringing salvation to all men, instructing us to deny ungodliness and worldly desires and to live sensibly, righteously and godly in the present age, looking for the blessed hope and the appearing of the glory of our great God and Savior, Christ Jesus, who gave Himself for us to redeem us from every lawless deed, and to purify for Himself a people for His own possession, zealous for good deeds.

God's grace brings His rescue from our sins. It also instructs us to turn away from sin each day. It teaches us to live in a way that God likes in a world that basically doesn't like God. It reminds us to wait for Jesus' second coming. It connects us with Jesus who has bought us out of our heart-slavery to wrong living and cleans us up like bleach on the inside so that we are unstoppable when it comes to doing good!

That sure doesn't sound like a passive, lazy, "Who cares?" view of life. No. Real grace, God's grace, is the greatest heart motivator to right living. Let me say it again: God's grace motivates us to right living. It did for Brian. Grace gave him the capacity to forgive. And grace gave him the "want to" and "power to" love his brother from the heart, resulting in action (spending time with his brother).

Grace was also the deep, inner motivator and core-level power for the apostle Paul. He wrote in 1 Corinthians 15:10:

> But by the grace of God I am what I am, and His grace toward me did not prove vain; but I labored even more than all of them, yet not I, but the grace of God with me.

So, can we bury forever the lie that living by grace will make for soft, wimpy, passive, do-nothing Christians? Personally, I think I know where that lie came from, since we have an enemy that is scared to death of God's true grace.

God's grace works. God's grace, in fact, *labors*. Not to attain, gain or maintain God's love or approval, but because we already have it in Christ.

A THOUGHT TO CHEW ON

God's grace is the greatest heart motivator to living right.

A TRUTH TO REMEMBER

"For the grace of God has appeared… instructing us to deny ungodliness and worldly desires and to live sensibly, righteously and godly in the present age" (Titus 2:11–12).

A QUESTION TO MULL OVER

How does experiencing and living by God's grace move us to do what is right in a way that is far more effective than simply being told what to do and what not to do?

TALKING IT OVER WITH GOD

Dear Father, it seems like there is a principle of life at work here, and that is that we can only express what we have already experienced. We can't show mercy if we haven't received mercy. We can't tell others the truth unless we have first heard and believed the truth ourselves. And we can't express grace until we have experienced it. Maybe that's why so many people try to motivate others with un-grace or even with dis-grace. One thing is clear: Your grace is dynamic, like dynamite. It is life-changing. It is heart-melting. It is right-living-empowering. It teaches us far better than guilt or shame motivation ever could.

So why is it that so often I still try to motivate and energize myself and others to right living by the wrong methods? I think my earlier words in this prayer are convicting me. The reason is that I am still only in kindergarten when it comes to experiencing Your grace and so I am too often still a preschooler when it comes to expressing it. But I do know that I have already been introduced to Your grace and in it I now stand.

So teach me how to grow in the grace and knowledge of Jesus, and in so doing, I know I will work – and work hard – in a way that accomplishes Your will and not mine. Amen.

Day 7: What's Love Got to Do with It?

My friend Daniel and I decided to go where (almost) no white men had gone before. It was a dangerous part of town called Casablanca. We were going there because we wanted to spread the good news of how Jesus changes lives, but we had no idea what would happen when we set foot in that neighborhood.

We did know that this area was better known for drug deals and gang shootings than spiritual life, so we prayed hard as we walked down the street. Clearly our presence was going to attract attention, arouse curiosity and likely cause suspicion. Had we not known that we were going at the direction of the Lord, we would have been scared.

Hoping to find someone who spoke English, we knocked on the door of a small, tan, ranch-style home, explaining that we had come to talk about Jesus. The woman of the house answered and gestured across the street. Her teenage daughter, Maria, who spoke English, was apparently there visiting a friend. The woman's two younger daughters raced across the street to fetch her. Our coming was something of a special occasion and the whole household came alive with laughter and conversation – none of which we could understand!

I'm sure eyes must have been peeking out from behind curtains up and down the block. And I'm sure Maria was wondering why in the world two white men wanted her.

When she crossed the street to where we were standing, we asked Maria if she was interested in talking about spiritual things. She kind of smiled and shook her head "No."

"In my church it is a sin to dance," she said, a bit angrily.

Out of the corner of my eye I spotted a rosebush where a beautiful yellow rose was blooming. It was in her front yard, so I motioned for Maria to follow me as I walked toward the bush.

"Maria, the issue is not dancing or not dancing. The issue is: Will you open your heart to Jesus so that He can clean you out and forgive you on the inside? Look at this rose. Just as this beautiful flower opened from a bud, so God wants to take your life and make it blossom. Could you trust in a God like that?"

After pausing to think for a moment, Maria nodded. After explaining in more depth what it means to open your heart to Christ, I asked her if she would like to do that. She said she would.

At my invitation, the three of us kneeled in her front yard. As I look back on that moment, I'm not sure why I did that. I've never done that since, and it isn't necessary to get on your knees to pray, but somehow at that moment it seemed like the right thing. It certainly kept her decision for Christ from being a hidden, private matter. The whole neighborhood had a front-row seat!

Daniel and I had the privilege of listening to Maria pray one of the most beautiful prayers I've ever heard as she opened her heart to Jesus.

Her younger sisters, who had already put their faith in Christ, were jumping up and down for joy. It turned out that Maria's mother and aunt (who lived with them) were Christians as well. So I told Maria to go inside the house and tell them what she had done.

Maria came out a few minutes later, describing how her aunt had hugged her and how her mother had said, "This is what we have been waiting for all your life!"

Daniel and I were beside ourselves with joy. We were able to take some time to encourage Maria in her new faith, but then it was time for us to leave.

As we started walking away, Maria called after us, "You guys are angels, aren't you?"

I smiled and called back, "No, Maria, we *are* God's messengers, but we are people just like you."

She didn't seem convinced. We walked on a little farther and she called out louder this time, "I know you guys are angels!"

Daniel and I laughed as I told him I had this urge to flap my arms like wings, but we just kept walking, grateful for a God who loves people so much that He would send us on such a cool assignment.

Sadly, too often Christians are known more for what they are *against* rather than for their *love*. But love is meant to be the most recognizable characteristic of those who follow Jesus. Jesus Himself said so:

> A new commandment I give to you, that you love one another, even as I have loved you, that you also love one another. By this all men will know that you are My disciples, if you have love for one another.
>
> John 13:34–35

Even as I write these words, I know there will be some who will read the last couple of paragraphs, and who will run and grab their "Yeah but" guns, and come running back with flushed faces, huffing and puffing, firing away. They'll excitedly shout, "Yeah, but you need truth as well! You need to take a stand against sin!"

Of course we need truth. And of course we need to stand against sin. God's love isn't wimpy and wishy-washy, and it never operates independently of God's truth, as 1 Corinthians 13:4–8 clearly teaches:

> Love is patient, love is kind and is not jealous; love does not brag and is not arrogant, does not act unbecomingly; it does not seek its own, is not provoked, does not

take into account a wrong suffered, *does not rejoice in unrighteousness, but rejoices with the truth;* bears all things, believes all things, hopes all things, endures all things. Love never fails… [emphasis mine].

But look at the words from 1 Corinthians 13 closely. Basically it's saying that while never compromising on the truth, love doesn't act like a jerk either. It is patient and kind and doesn't act like it always has all the answers. It isn't rude or disrespectful and doesn't act in a self-centered way, doesn't fly off the handle and doesn't allow past wounds to dictate present actions.

In other words, love is full of grace because love – the real love of Christ – is from God (1 John 4:7). And God is love (1 John 4:8). And God is gracious.

So, in answer to the question posed by the title of today's reading, when it comes to grace, love – God's love, that is – has *everything* to do with it.

A THOUGHT TO CHEW ON

Love is meant to be the most recognizable characteristic of those who follow Jesus.

A TRUTH TO REMEMBER

"By this all men will know that you are My disciples, if you have love for one another" (John 13:35).

A QUESTION TO MULL OVER

Take a look at the qualities of God's love in 1 Corinthians 13:4–8. How well do your life and character reflect those qualities? Are you more defined by what you are *against* or by the deep love that you demonstrate to those around you, especially those with whom you differ?

TALKING IT OVER WITH GOD

Dear Father, left to my own instincts and inclinations, I admit that I find it much easier to be angry than patient; harsh rather than kind; riding my own high horse instead of humbly serving others. I don't want to be rude or critical but it is easy to slip into that mode, even becoming smugly self-satisfied by my own sharp tongue and clever put-downs. I'm afraid I nurse grudges too often and rejoice in the downfall of others with whom I disagree instead of being there to catch them when they fall. Jesus was called the friend of sinners and I want to be like Him. I need Your love, Lord. No, what I really need is You, Lord, because You are love. Would You please take my character which, if I am honest, is not always very gracious, and mold me into a patient, kind, caring, gracious, loving person, so that when people look at me they would know that I am Your disciple. Not so that I would get any credit, but so that people who had not considered You as relevant, might take a second look. Amen.

Canceling the Guilt Trip

Day 8: Busted!

During this second week we are going to focus on the subject of guilt and how God's grace rescues us from that "spiritual quicksand." An important principle of this week's readings is for us to understand that guilt has actually nothing to do with our feelings. That may come as a surprise or even a shock to you, because many people determine whether they *are* guilty by whether they *feel* guilty. That is, they confuse "guilt" with "guilt feelings." This confusion will get you nowhere fast, as we will see during the course of this week.

Allow me a moment of cultural commentary, but I have observed a slow and subtle but very real shift over the past thirty years or so in terms of how people determine what truth is. I can especially see it in how my parents talk about things versus how my children do. My generation – the one in between those two – seems to be the transition zone. Let me explain.

Ask a senior adult a question like, "Who is going to win the upcoming election?" Their answer will be something like, "I believe 'so and so' will win" or "I don't think 'what's his name' stands a chance." But ask one of my kids the same question and they will respond, "I feel like 'blah blah blah' is going to win." My generation could express it either way.

See the difference? Now, both ultimately are giving an opinion, but the younger generation tends to consult their feelings to determine what is true for them, which is spiritually dangerous territory. Why is that? Well, when it comes to what God says, the word of God is true whether we feel it is true or not. And if someone is struggling to believe the Bible, it could very well be that deep down they have believed the lie that "what I feel is true must be true", as opposed to what the facts of the word of God say.

This is a real problem because our faith is meant to be based on who God is and what He declares is truth (objective reality), as opposed to whether we "feel" something is true (subjective perception) or even whether we are "convicted" of something being wrong. Let me illustrate.

A number of years ago I was living in Ohio, training a younger guy for ministry. One evening we were both headed to a particular church for a meeting. Marv (not his real name) was convinced a particular route was faster. I disagreed. We decided to have a healthy competition – a race, if you will – though the ground rules required not exceeding the speed limit. Marv went his way and I went mine.

As I was driving along, the thought entered my mind that Marv had to be speeding. He was too much of a competitor to lose this race, and so, being competitive myself, I increased my speed from 35 to 45 mph – 10 mph over the speed limit. No big deal, I thought.

It couldn't have been a minute later that a police car passing me going the opposite direction made a U-turn, turned on its lights and rushed up on my tail. I groaned, rolled my eyes and, knowing I was busted, pulled over. Of course, the police officer took his good old time before getting out of his vehicle and coming over to my driver's-side window. By that time I knew I had lost the race and, as I sat there frustrated, the Lord took the opportunity to remind me of Romans 13, which instructs us to obey the governing authorities... including traffic laws. I was pretty deflated by the time the policeman presented me with the ticket.

"I clocked you doing 45 in a 35 zone," the officer stated flatly.

"Sir, I want to thank you for being an instrument of God. That's what the Bible calls you. I was wrong and God wanted me to know that I can't get away with breaking the law, so I got caught. Thanks."

I was actually sincere in what I said, but I'm sure the policeman thought he had some kind of religious nutcase on his hands! Either that or he added my comments to his mental register of "now I've heard everything." I'm sure he and his buddies had a good laugh about it back at the station.

Either way, it didn't change his mind. I still got the ticket. All I could think about was how much this fine was going to hurt my cash flow and how happy Marv would be for winning. I was not happy.

When I finally walked – quite late – into the church meeting, Marv looked up at me with a puzzled expression.

"I got pulled over for speeding," I whispered, a bit disgusted at the smug smile spreading across his victorious face. "You were speeding too, weren't you?" I said, irritated that there was not the slightest hint of remorse on Marv's face as he nodded triumphantly.

Who was guilty? Just the one who got caught? What about the one who was speeding but didn't get caught and didn't feel the least bit guilty about breaking the law – not to mention the rules of the game?! Was he guilty?

Actually, both of us were guilty, though God chose to hold me accountable for my wrongdoing, probably because there is always a stricter judgment for us teachers (see James 3:1).

Guilt is a legal condition of being in the wrong and being held accountable for that wrongdoing by a human or divine court of law. Guilt before a human court of law typically results in some form of punishment – either the paying of a fine (like I had to pay for speeding) or the doing of community service or some sort of restriction (like probation) or confinement (imprisonment).

But what about the divine court? What is God's role in determining and punishing our guilt? In order for us to ultimately understand and appreciate *God's grace*, we first must recognize *God's justice*. That's worth repeating. *In order for us to grasp hold of the grace of God with gratitude, we first must face the tough reality of the justice of God.*

The fact that God is a Judge is a theme that is found throughout the Bible. For example, King David wrote:

> The LORD judges the peoples;
> Vindicate me, O LORD, according to my righteousness
> and my integrity that is in me.
> O let the evil of the wicked come to an end, but establish
> the righteous;
> For the righteous God tries the hearts and minds.
> My shield is with God,
> Who saves the upright in heart.
> God is a righteous judge,
> And a God who has indignation every day.
>
> Psalm 7:8–11

James, in the New Testament, also reminds us that the God of grace is also the Judge:

> Do not complain, brethren, against one another, so that
> you yourselves may not be judged; behold, the Judge is
> standing right at the door.
>
> James 5:9

That's pretty clear. The God who is love and who is gracious is also a Judge who is angry at the evil that wicked men do and will "try" in His court of justice the hearts and minds of people. He is not being some kind of "cosmic meanie" when He does this. He is being righteous. In other words, He is doing what is right. And despite how it might seem at times, God does not turn a blind eye or a deaf ear to wrongdoing. He is very aware of what is going on and will one day come to fully execute justice. For anyone who has ever been abused, betrayed, abandoned, victimized by crime, or persecuted, or has in any way suffered at the hands of cruel and uncaring people, this is very good news.

Now, at this point, we hope that you are not getting confused. Back in Day 2 we asked the question, "Is God gracious?" And we responded to our own question with a resounding "YES!" Don't worry. God hasn't pulled a fast one and changed between Day 2 and Day 8! He is still gracious and will always be gracious. *But once again, grace cannot be fully understood or appreciated except against the backdrop of justice.*

Justice could be defined as God giving us what we deserve (which is punishment for our sin and guilt). Mercy would then be defined as God *not* giving us what we deserve (that is, withholding punishment for our sin and guilt). What is grace, then? Grace is God giving us what we *don't* deserve (which is forgiveness, life and relationship with Him despite our wrongdoing).

So… let's go back to our discussion of God's justice for just a few more minutes.

Doesn't it seem sometimes like those who do evil get off scot-free? I mean, look at the brutal dictators who commit genocide. They live in vast, plush palaces and seem to be beyond the reach of justice. And what about drug cartel leaders who are raking in multi-millions while the drugs they control destroy the lives of thousands? They protect themselves with armed men and live in the lap of luxury at the expense of the rest of humanity.

Where is the God of justice?

The answer to that question is that He is on His throne, and one day He will sit as Judge of the whole earth, and it will be all over for the wicked. Check out what Isaiah 2 has to say:

> For the LORD of hosts will have a day of reckoning
> Against everyone who is proud and lofty
> And against everyone who is lifted up,
> That he may be abased...
> The pride of man will be humbled
> And the loftiness of men will be abased;
> And the LORD alone will be exalted in that day,
> But the idols will completely vanish.
> Men will go into caves of the rocks
> And into holes of the ground
> Before the terror of the LORD
> And the splendor of His majesty,
> When He arises to make the earth tremble.
>
> Isaiah 2:12, 17–19

So, here's the big question: Who is in the crosshairs of God's justice? And how do those who are guilty before such a holy God escape judgment and enter into this place of mercy and grace that we talked about in Week 1?

Remember, the issue is not "Do I *feel* guilty?" but "*Am* I guilty?" If you are asking that question, you should be really ready for some good news. Stay tuned...

A THOUGHT TO CHEW ON

Guilt is not a matter of *feelings*, but a matter of *fact*.

A TRUTH TO REMEMBER

"God is a righteous judge, and a God who has indignation every day" (Psalm 7:11).

A QUESTION TO MULL OVER

Why do you think it is important to grasp at some level the justice of God in order to appreciate the grace of God?

TALKING IT OVER WITH GOD

Dear Father, in one sense I'm really glad that You are a Judge because there is sure a lot of injustice in the world. All the people who have never received the justice due here on earth will one day get it. Your word says that "judgment will be merciless to one that has shown no mercy" (James 2:13). That makes this insane world a bit easier to take, though it makes me wonder how merciful I have been.

It is mind-boggling to realize that there isn't one scrap of wrongdoing that You haven't seen, and that You see it with perfect clarity… never being faked out by anyone's lies or schemes or hidden motives. Because You are a completely wise God, You will treat each case and each circumstance with absolutely perfect justice. But the fact that You never miss a single thing kind of scares me. What will You say to me when I see You face to face? Will I truly escape Your judgment or do You have a bone to pick with me that will spoil the whole deal?

I do find comfort in reading that "the Lord is full of compassion and is merciful" (James 5:11). Help me to balance these seemingly conflicting aspects of Your character – justice and grace – so that I can find peace in my heart and rest for my soul. Amen.

Day 9: The Way Home

I think it's really cool when movies or scenes in movies illustrate truths about life and our relationship with God. One of those movies, based on a true-life incident, is *Apollo 13*, starring Tom Hanks as mission commander, Jim Lovell. The Apollo 13 flight was to be highlighted by achieving the third lunar landing by an American spacecraft. That aspect of the mission had to be aborted when an explosion ruptured oxygen tank no. 2 in the service module and also ruptured a line or damaged a valve in the no. 1 oxygen tank, causing it to lose oxygen fast. The service module bay no. 4 cover was blown off. All the supplies of oxygen were lost within about three hours, along with loss of water, electrical power, and use of the propulsion system. It was a mess.

This crisis gave rise to the now famous line, "Houston, we have a problem." And what had at first been viewed by the American public as just another trip to the moon, suddenly became a national and global drama. Was there any way the three men in that spacecraft would make it safely home?

In the movie, the suspense builds as they realize that time is not on their side. The carbon dioxide in the cabin is rising to a dangerous level and one of the crew becomes seriously ill with a kidney infection. Then, to make matters worse, the men are basically on their own as they navigate through the earth's atmosphere. Their high-tech guidance equipment is useless.

Rocketing through space toward planet earth at thousands of miles per hour, they must enter the atmosphere at precisely the correct angle. If the angle is wrong, they will either burn up like a shooting star or skip off earth's atmosphere back into space like a rock skimming off a pond. The powerful gravitational pull of earth would either draw them home to safety or send them to their deaths. One way or the other, they had an appointment with planet earth that could not be stopped and would not be easy.

So what's the point? Good question. After all, you didn't pick up today's devotional to read a movie review – especially an old, 1995 movie review.

Here's the tie-in between the film, *Apollo 13*, and our relationship with God: God's love draws us toward Him with a power as magnetic as the earth's gravity pulling on that spacecraft. And God is "not wishing for any to perish but for all to come to repentance" (2 Peter 3:9).

God really and truly desires that everyone would come home to His safe, saving presence, but there is a barrier – another aspect of His perfect character – that causes a problem for all mankind, not just Houston. It is His holiness and justice. Because of His holiness, God hates man's sin – yours and mine included – and because of His justice, that sin must be punished. Apart from Christ, we are guilty as charged and "the wages of sin is death" (Romans 6:23). The apostle John expresses God's holiness this way:

God is Light, and in Him there is no darkness at all.

1 John 1:5

As humans without Christ, we are darkness and in us there is no light at all.

God is pure; apart from Christ we are not. God is incapable of sin; we are born into it. God cannot even be tempted by sin (James 1:13); we give in to temptation many times without even batting an eyelash. God's eyes are too holy to look upon or tolerate evil (Habakkuk 1:13); we too often drool over it. Someone has to give. And I'll give you a hint: It's not God. We have to come to God on His terms, not ours.

But in another sense, God *is* the One who gives, "For God so loved the world, that He *gave* His only begotten Son, that whoever believes in Him shall not perish, but have eternal life" (John 3:16, emphasis mine).

Jesus alone is the way to safety with God, the highway to the Father in heaven.

The two options for Apollo 13 if it missed the one way home were both deadly. Either burn up with fire in the earth's atmosphere or suffocate in the darkness of outer space. Either way, the result was the same. With a solemn warning, the Bible speaks of eternal punishment for those who reject or miss Jesus. Hell is described both as a place of unquenchable fire and as an "outer darkness."

Just as there was only one precise way for the Apollo 13 spacecraft to make it through earth's atmosphere, so there is only one way to a holy, loving God: Jesus. He said it Himself: "I am the way, and the truth, and the life; no one comes to the Father but through Me" (John 14:6).

Notice that Jesus did not say He was *a* way or *one of many* ways. He said He was, and is, *the* way.

Jesus is the Father's solution to the dilemma (to us, not to God!) of how to satisfy His holiness and justice in not excusing our sin and guilt, while also providing us the way home to Him. Here's how the Bible writer, Paul, put it:

> For everyone has sinned; we all fall short of God's glorious standard. Yet God, with undeserved kindness [grace], declares that we are righteous. He did this through Christ Jesus when he freed us from the penalty for our sins. For God presented Jesus as the sacrifice for sin. People are made right with God when they believe that Jesus sacrificed his life, shedding his blood. This sacrifice shows that God was being fair when he held back and did not punish those who sinned in times past, for he was looking ahead and

including them in what he would do in this present time.
God did this to demonstrate his righteousness, for he
himself is fair and just, and he declares sinners to be right in
his sight when they believe in Jesus.

Romans 3:23–26 NLT

Through Christ, God is both just (right and fair) and the justifier (the One who makes us right and innocent) of the one who puts his or her faith in Jesus. So when all is said and done, God is not guilty and neither are we!

One final connection to the voyage of Apollo 13 is worth mentioning.

The spacecraft was necessary for the three men to make it safely home. As long as they remained in the *Odyssey*, Apollo 13's command and service module, they were OK. They were safe. The spacecraft, however, didn't fare so well. Its outside was scorched, battered and beaten up.

So was Jesus. He was beaten, broken and battered, and then He died. And even though He was raised totally victorious from the dead, He still bears the scars of His journey. Those marks on His body will be an eternal reminder that the rescue from sin that costs us nothing cost Jesus everything. The highway to God was not paved without pain; the highway to heaven was built with blood... the blood of Christ.

But the good news is that everyone who is *in Christ* comes home safe and sound.

A THOUGHT TO CHEW ON

Jesus is the only way to be rescued and safe from sin and guilt.

A TRUTH TO REMEMBER

"[God is] just and the justifier of the one who has faith in Jesus" (Romans 3:26).

A QUESTION TO MULL OVER

Do you believe that Jesus is the only way to God? Or does it seem a bit narrow and unfair to you for God to do things that way? Why or why not?

TALKING IT OVER WITH GOD

Dear Father, sometimes I wonder about those who have never had the chance to hear about Jesus, and I worry about where they will end up. I know You have told us to go tell them, but ultimately I have to leave that matter in Your hands. The Bible says You are both just and the justifier of the one who has faith in Jesus, so however You handle that matter must be fair.

I guess the even scarier question is, "What about all those who have heard and, as of now, do not believe?" Help me to have the courage to urge people to come to You now while they have the chance, and also make sure that I know that I know that I know You.

You are so kind and good to provide the way to safety with You in Christ, and He is so great to have gone through so much so that I could be innocent, safe and sound in Him. Thank You! Amen.

Day 10: The Grace Club

Sometimes the best way to learn to appreciate something is to experience the exact opposite for a while. Do you want to have a new appreciation for food? Try fasting for three or four days and a cracker will taste like a gourmet meal. Think about the last time you were really sick... maybe with the flu that wiped you out for a few weeks. Do you remember how good it felt to be healthy again?

In this week, remember that we are looking at how God takes us out of the humanly desperate condition of guilt and declares us innocent by His grace through our faith in Jesus. Is that realization still fresh on your heart or have you come to take being in a state of forgiveness for granted? It's easy to do that, especially if it was quite a while ago that you first came into relationship with God through Christ. Maybe you need, like I did, a short refresher course on the desperation of guilt in order to celebrate the delight of grace again.

I hope the real-life drama in today's reading will help you to remember, as it helped me to do so. It takes place in the Philippines where I was privileged to have worked in the same ministry as the remarkable man in this story. Let me introduce you to Tom and his very personal story about guilt and forgiveness.[3]

Directed by God to face some very deep pain in his life, Tom walked into the prison cell and looked into the face of the man who had murdered his older brother in cold blood. As is often the case with boys, Tom had grown up admiring, even idolizing, his older brother.

The murderer, depressed and weary, confessed that all he wanted to do was find a priest to pray with him so he could die. Instead, Tom and his friend, a man in the military, brought him life. They shared the good news of Jesus Christ and His forgiveness. After a very fierce battle with the powers of darkness (the prisoner had been heavily involved with the occult), the man knew he needed and wanted the Lord. With great difficulty, he was finally able to cry out, "Jesus… save me!"

Instantly the man's stiff and convulsing body went limp and his agonized face grew soft. Christ had rescued him and set him free! Realizing what had happened, this new follower of Jesus leaped to his feet and began dancing and clapping his hands like a little child – right there in his jail cell! He praised God and told the evil spirits to "Get lost!" in the name of Jesus.

As the two men prepared to leave, the new believer asked for their names. The military officer first introduced himself and then the man with him, Tom Roxas (pronounced like "Ro-hahs").

"Roxas?!" The man gasped at the familiar family name, reeling back. The prisoner suddenly realized that he had killed Tom's older brother. The victim had been a journalist, murdered because he was doing research for an exposé on organized crime in Manila.

"Yes, he is the brother of the man you killed," Tom's friend confirmed.

Suddenly the prisoner fell to the ground, his face at Tom's feet, sobbing, "Forgive me, forgive me!"

Tom knelt, lifted him up, and looked at him, saying, "Christ has forgiven me, and I also have forgiven you." In a rush of emotion, they hugged, wept for joy and praised God together… as brothers.

A few days later, Tom and his friend visited their new brother to assure him again of his salvation. "I couldn't look into your eyes previously," the prisoner confessed. "If I were in your place my blood would boil. Christ surely must be in you, for no ordinary man could forgive me as you have."

The new believer went on to assure Tom and his friend that he knew that the same Christ lived in him. He had already joyfully shared the good news of hope and forgiveness with another cellmate.

What an incredible story... and totally true. A guilty murderer is pardoned for eternity by the Righteous Judge, the Lord Jesus Christ. And thus a prisoner behind bars for the rest of his life is set free – more free than many walking around outside those same prison walls.

It is easy to be touched by this level of forgiveness by God (and Tom!) toward such a guilty, hopeless man. After all, a cold-blooded murderer is about as low as you can go, especially when the one killed is a righteous man.

But what about you and me? Chances are, you are not reading this devotional while behind bars (though if you are, I hope you find great encouragement!). You may, like me, look back at your life and recall incidents in which you lied or spoke harshly, hatefully and hurtfully. Maybe you abandoned a relationship and left somebody battered and broken. But by and large, we don't view ourselves as being all that bad, do we?

Have you ever gotten angry with someone? Have you ever lost your temper and called somebody a nasty name? Have you ever put somebody down and openly, publicly humiliated them? If so, welcome to the club.

Though we might shrug our shoulders and think, "Well, nobody's perfect!", Jesus told us that losing our cool is actually serious stuff. Here's what He said:

> You have heard that the ancients were told, "You shall
> not commit murder" and "Whoever commits murder
> shall be liable to the court." But I say to you that
> everyone who is angry with his brother shall be guilty
> before the court; and whoever says to his brother, "You

good-for-nothing," shall be guilty before the supreme court; and whoever says, "You fool," shall be guilty enough to go into the fiery hell.

Matthew 5:21–22

Heavy stuff, huh? I mean, at first glance, apart from Christ I can easily see that Tom Roxas' brother's murderer deserved to go to hell, but certainly not me!? What's the big deal anyway? After all, everybody gets mad once in a while, right? But when I look closely at what Jesus said and honestly face the anger and hatred that used to fill my life before Christ, I have to admit I can see myself being ushered into the same cell as the cold-blooded murderer in prison... in as much need of God's forgiving grace as he was. Can you?

The apostle Paul seemed to be driving home that same point in Romans 3:9–12:

> What then? Are we better than they? Not at all; for we
> have already charged that both Jews and Greeks are all
> under sin; as it is written,
> There is none righteous, not even one;
> There is none who understands,
> There is none who seeks for God;
> All have turned aside, together they have become
>   useless;
> There is none who does good,
> There is not even one.

Do you find a defensiveness rising in your heart at these words? Do you feel compelled to object that these words are too harsh an indictment of a human soul? Are you finding yourself throwing all your weight against the word of God that would seek to cast "the pre-Christian you" into the same cell as Tom Roxas' brother's murderer?

It's hard to face the truth sometimes.

As good as we may have thought we were, apart from Christ none of us sought after God. Dead men can't seek anything. And all of us were (spiritually) dead in our sins (Ephesians 2:1). We were separated from the life of God, with no hope of ever finding Him on our own.

But God…

Those may be the two most marvelous words in the Bible.

> But God, being rich in mercy, because of His great love with which He loved us, even when we were dead in our transgressions, made us alive together with Christ (by grace you have been saved), and raised us up with Him, and seated us with Him in the heavenly places in Christ Jesus, so that in the ages to come He might show the surpassing riches of His grace in kindness toward us in Christ Jesus.
>
> Ephesians 2:4–7

We were lost.
God sought us out.
We were dead.
God gave us life so that we could respond to His call to
    come to Him.
We were unable to save ourselves.
God rescued us by His grace.
We were in prison, on death row.
God raised us up and set us free.
We were alone, abandoned, helpless and hopeless.
God brought us to heaven to sit next to Him so that
throughout the rest of eternity He could love us and hug
us and pour out acts of kindness on us in Christ.

The LORD sets the prisoners free.

> Psalm 146:7b

Welcome to the club... not the Club of the Condemned, but the Club of Condemned Criminals Set Free by God's Grace.

A THOUGHT TO CHEW ON

Apart from Christ, every one of us was a condemned criminal.

A TRUTH TO REMEMBER

"But God..." (Ephesians 2:4).

A QUESTION TO MULL OVER

Do you have the assurance in your heart that you have been forgiven and rescued from sin's penalty through Christ? If your answer is yes, how do you know? If you don't, what do you need to do today to get out of that jail cell of guilt?

TALKING IT OVER WITH GOD

Dear Father, it's easy over time to forget how desperately hopeless my soul's condition was before You rescued me. The memories of Your mercy and gratitude for Your grace can both fade over the years. Maybe that's why the apostle Paul — even though he knew he was a redeemed child of God, a saint — still referred to himself as the chief of sinners. He never wanted to forget how utterly guilty and lost he was without You and how completely undeserving of Your rescuing grace he was.

Lord, as uncomfortable as it makes me feel, I willingly acknowledge that apart from Christ I was that cold-blooded killer's roommate in prison. But I thank You that I'm not there anymore. Through Your grace and my faith in Jesus alone to forgive me, You have set me free from guilt and now I am innocent of all charges. What a relief!

Please help this recognition of Your amazing grace to not wane, but instead to grow stronger and stronger every day until I can finally thank You face to face. I can't wait! Amen.

Day 11: The Hammer Fell

I know what it's like to feel guilty. About a year and a half after I had become a follower of Christ, I was celebrating my twentieth birthday with my college buddies in one of their rooms on my dorm floor. I had been drinking pretty heavily throughout that springtime evening when the alarm sounded from one of my friends: "Your brother is coming down the hall!" It might as well have been the apostle Peter as far as I was concerned.

My brother had been the first one to tell me about Jesus and he was a sincere and steady follower of the Lord. I was definitely struggling spiritually. I quickly hid my bottle of beer and tried to look sober. Have you ever tried to look sober when you are almost sloshed? Good luck. You might as well try to not look pregnant at eight months!

When my brother walked in, his bright face immediately fell. I could read disappointment all over it.

"Happy birthday, Rich," my brother said, with as cheery a voice as he was able to muster.

Sort of awkwardly, he handed me a gift. It was a book. I dreaded opening it, suspecting things were about to go from bad to worse. My fears were realized when I opened it and saw that it was *The Master Plan of Evangelism* by Robert Coleman. My partying friends were a bit amused by the whole scene, as I had never made much of an effort to tell them about my faith, though they knew I was a Christian. I wanted to crawl into a hole.

Mercifully, my brother left quickly. The horrible guilt feelings I experienced were soon drowned in a few more bottles of brew. By around 11 p.m. I was drunk.

My friends, sensing an opportunity to take advantage of my helpless condition, wrapped me in a bed sheet and carried me off to the dormitory elevator. Pushing all the buttons (to make sure I would make a grand appearance on each of the eight floors), they closed the elevator doors and went off to party some more.

The guilt and shame came flooding back when I reached each floor and had to deal with all the pointing, taunts and laughter. To make matters worse, I was starting to feel really sick.

Somehow I was able to maneuver out of the elevator when it got back to my floor, and I crawled out and curled up in a corner of the fourth-floor lobby to sleep. I was really pathetic. A while later I woke up and by that time was feeling so nauseous that I think I made a vow to become a priest or something if God kept me from vomiting.

Over time I inched my way down the hall toward my room, knocking on various doors, hoping for help. Nobody was around. After probably an hour or so I made it back to my room. My roommate was in bed but not asleep.

"Oh no," I thought. "Here comes the sermon." If my brother were the apostle Peter, my roommate was the apostle Bob. Bob was his name. I waited for the hammer to fall.

Suddenly, my buddies came crashing into the room. Noticing that my feet and lower legs were hanging off the foot of the bed, they grabbed my ankles and heaved my body forward, driving my head into the wall. I should have been in agony, but I felt nothing.

Probably assuming that I was dead and therefore no more fun, my friends left me alone with my roommate. If guilt were sweat, my clothes would have been drenched. I wondered what my roommate was about to say. I readied myself with a quick rebuttal, prepared to lash back if I received a harsh scolding or convicting lecture.

All he quietly said was, "Do you really think this is glorifying God?" And then he went to sleep.

But I didn't. I couldn't. As a follower of Christ I should have known better. I *did* know better. But I didn't know how to get back to being close to Jesus.

In the days following, I could easily have been swallowed up in the quicksand of guilt and shame, but I wasn't. Even in the midst of my sin, twice in one night I had come face to face with grace and, though I didn't realize it at the time, grace was about to take me by the hand and walk me back to Jesus that summer.

Depending on their church background and training, some people would be quick to draw one or more of the following conclusions about my story:

1. Well, he may have *thought* he was a Christian at that time, but based on how he was living, it's clear he wasn't.

2. His brother and roommate really missed the boat. They should have laid down the law with him for his drunkenness and taught him a lesson he'd not soon forget!

3. I bet God really gave him a good spanking for that sorry behavior!

The spirit behind those kinds of comments was what I was expecting from my brother and roommate, to be perfectly honest. But there was a different spirit demonstrated. It was a spirit of grace.

For some reading this devotional, it will come as a surprise to know that prior to that birthday party there was no question that I had trusted in Jesus to forgive me and that I was in Christ and Christ was in me. Was I walking with the Lord at the time of this sad tale, keeping in step with His Spirit? Clearly not. But relationally, I was God's child. My drinking too much did not change that.

How, then, did God view me and my sin that night? Let's take a look at several scriptures:

> He [God] predestined us to adoption as sons through Jesus Christ to Himself, according to the kind intention of His will, to the praise of the glory of His grace, which He freely bestowed on us in the Beloved. In Him we have redemption through His blood, the forgiveness of our trespasses, according to the riches of His grace which He lavished on us.
>
> Ephesians 1:5–8a

> For He rescued us from the domain of darkness, and transferred us to the kingdom of His beloved Son, in whom we have redemption, the forgiveness of sins.
>
> Colossians 1:13–14

> When you were dead in your transgressions and the uncircumcision of your flesh, He made you alive together with Him, having forgiven us all our transgressions, having canceled out the certificate of debt consisting of decrees against us, which was hostile to us; and He has taken it out of the way, having nailed it to the cross.
>
> Colossians 2:13–14

Based on these scriptures, there are some things very clear about how God viewed me and my sin that night. And, by the way, since all of us sin, even after we come to know Jesus, this is how He views you and your sin as well!

First, I was God's adopted child before I sinned. I was God's adopted child after I sinned. Nothing changed relationally with the Father and me when I sinned.

Second, I was no longer a part of the domain of darkness;

I had been smuggled out of that dark place and brought into Jesus' kingdom. My behavior, then, was inconsistent with who I was. I didn't know that at the time, and that was part of the problem. But God knew, and He was lovingly determined to teach me how to live rightly in His kingdom, as a saint, a child of God.

Third, when Christ died, the whole nasty list of my nasty sins was nailed to the cross where Jesus paid it all. My sins of drunkenness and rebellion against His leadership were on that list. I was already forgiven for those sins before I even committed them!

Fourth, the brief glimpses of grace that my brother and roommate showed me were just that – brief glimmers of the incredibly vast flood of grace that God lavished on me then, lavishes on me now and will continue to lavish on me unconditionally throughout my entire life.

Later this week we will look more closely at *guilt feelings* and what those really are all about. But for now, if you are in Christ and Christ is in you, the verdict rendered on your life, even when you sin, is NOT GUILTY by virtue of Jesus suffering and dying in your place and your faith in Him alone to forgive you.

It is not just your past sins that are forgiven in Christ. They were all in the future when Christ died. No, your past sins, your present sins, your future sins have all been forgiven in Christ. Remember, Colossians 2:13 above says that He has "forgiven *all* your transgressions." All means all. Not some. Not most. Not just the ones you committed before you opened your heart to Christ. Not just the ones you remember to confess. All.

You are righteous. You are holy. You are forgiven. You are alive. You are not guilty.

So many of us are waiting for the hammer to fall…

waiting for God to strike us down for our sins. Child of God, the hammer already fell. It fell on Christ. What falls on you now is God's grace: grace to change, grace to do what's right, grace to believe that God really loves you – yes, you – even when you sin.

A THOUGHT TO CHEW ON

In Christ, your guilt has been taken away. You are NOT GUILTY.

A TRUTH TO REMEMBER

"In Him we have redemption through His blood, the forgiveness of our trespasses, according to the riches of His grace which He lavished on us" (Ephesians 1:5–8a).

A QUESTION TO MULL OVER

Can it really be true that *all* your sins and my sins have been taken away from us in Christ and that we are really and truly completely forgiven? What kind of impact does that news have on you?

TALKING IT OVER WITH GOD

Dear Father, it seems like a lot of Your people as well as a lot of Your churches get some sort of distorted spiritual energy out of feeling guilty and making others feel guilty. It's as if it is the norm, the expected thing. Based on Your word, that is kind of creepy because the thing that makes the good news such good news is that guilt is really gone. Forgiveness is 100 percent complete. Jesus really did mean it on the cross when He cried out, "It is finished!"

The only alternative to this life of freedom in Your grace is some kind of works system by which we somehow have to keep our noses clean or perform really well religiously in order to stay in Your good graces. But Your word says that if the removal of our guilt is by works, it is no longer by grace, because then grace would no longer be grace (Romans 11:6). So either the work done for our rescue from sin is Your work or our work. It can't be both.

Thank You that being justified by Your grace, we have been made heirs according to the hope of eternal life (Titus 3:7). It is a relief to know that my sin can't screw up this system because Your grace is stronger than my sin. That doesn't make me want to sin more. It makes me want to live my life in a way that honors a God like You who would do that for me. Amen.

Day 12: Faithing the Facts of Forgiveness

OK. Hopefully by now you are getting the message. In Christ, guilt is gone – completely. Zero. Zilch. Nada. Guilt doesn't even enter into the equation with someone who is a true follower of Christ. We are, as this week's title declares, *innocent*! We are not under law, we are under grace. And grace is the great guilt-stain remover!

I know. I know. That seems hard to believe... too good to be true. But it is good and it is true. Just keep reading over and thinking about and praying through those Scripture verses that we have been pointing out this week. If the lights haven't come on yet, hang in there, they will.

I think part of our struggle with letting go of guilt is because somewhere along the way we come to a sort of weird conclusion like, "Yeah, that's probably true for other, better Christians, but somehow I don't think it applies to me." Maybe some of us don't really think it's possible that all our guilt is gone because we feel that what we have done is so bad. We have let God down so much (by the way, we were never holding Him up!) or we have deeply disappointed our parents or ourselves or... after all, we should've known better.

Could it be that your problem is not that God hasn't forgiven you (because if you are in Christ, He already has!) but that you haven't forgiven yourself?

Now to some, that may set off the alarms, flashing "Psychobabble Warning! Look out, here comes the fluffy counseling stuff!" Don't worry. I'm not going to tell you to find a group of people, hold hands, look in the mirror and chant, "I'm good enough. I'm smart enough. And doggone it, people like me!"... or something along those lines. That's not what I'm talking about.

Forgiving yourself is not about trying to overwhelm your negative self-talk with consistent, persistent, warm, fuzzy, self-flattering messages. Forgiving yourself is not a matter of faking the facts. It's about facing the facts… really, *faithing* the facts. That sounds like I'm lisping but I'm not.

I'll explain more about that in a minute, but first I am going to change the subject a bit. This might seem like a rabbit trail, but don't worry, it won't lead us down a rabbit hole! The "rabbit trail" takes us to a pool in Jerusalem called Bethesda and a lame man who had been lying there for thirty-eight years. Rumor had it that at certain random times an angel would stir up the waters of that pool and whoever jumped in the pool first could play Marco Polo. Just kidding… whoever jumped in the pool first would supposedly be healed.

Now it's hard to imagine God actually working that way – rewarding the person that was young enough or fast enough or not lame enough, so that he beat everybody else to the punch. But that's the story that was going around at the time.

Back to the lame man. He had an encounter with Jesus. Let's pick up the story:

> When Jesus saw him lying there, and knew that he had
> already been a long time in that condition, He said to
> him, "Do you wish to get well?"
>
> John 5:5–6

In a minute we'll see how the man responds, but as I'm listening to Jesus I'm having a hard time imagining a more stupid or offensive question. Can you imagine going into the cancer ward of a hospital and asking people if they would like to be cured? I'm picturing people's faces contorting with anger as they make sarcastic replies like, "Nah, I like being sick and miserable. It's really fun."

And yet, though Jesus' question may have been a bit offensive, it wasn't stupid. It cut to the heart. Jesus' questions always had a way of doing that.

> The sick man answered Him, "Sir, I have no man to put me into the pool when the water is stirred up, but while I am coming, another steps down before me."
>
> John 5:7

You gotta pity the guy... or maybe not. He had enough self-pity to go around. Still... thirty-eight years of coming in second place. Talk about bad luck. Watching everybody else get their miracle and coming within inches of your own and then missing out... again.

Makes me wonder a bit. Why did Jesus go to that man and no other? Why did He ask him that question? Is it possible that the man had gotten used to the idea of being lame? After all, with thirty-eight years of failure you could easily come to accept it as your lot in life, your identity. He likely was one of the elder statesmen of the pool of Bethesda, with many an exciting story to tell of near-miss miracles. Maybe he believed he didn't deserve to be healed because of some terrible sin he had committed. Later on, Jesus did say to him, "Behold, you have become well; do not sin anymore, so that nothing worse happens to you" (John 5:14).

Sometimes I think we can get in a similar situation. Because we have sinned we accept a sort of "second-class" Christian citizenship, thinking that a life of not-quite-being-forgiven is what we deserve... that it's our lot in life, our identity. And so we allow ourselves to be haunted by guilt feelings, accepting it as sort of our punishment... our penance for wrongdoing. Somehow we don't think we're worthy of fully receiving God's acquittal of our guilt because we have been so bad.

Sounds kind of noble, in a morbid sort of way, doesn't it?

Well, to finish our rabbit trail journey, you might be interested to know that Jesus didn't say to the guy, "Well, you loser, you're getting what you deserve. Your sin is so bad that you ought to do cartwheels for joy – if you could, though you can't, of course, because you're lame – you ought to be thankful you're even alive." No, Jesus said, "Get up, pick up your pallet and walk" (John 5:8).

Jesus healed him. End of rabbit trail story.

Now, I don't know where you are in your faith journey, but if you have really struggled with letting go of your guilt and believing (faithing!) God's truth of your forgiveness, maybe it's time for you to stop hanging around the pool of lousy excuses and get up and start walking. Sorry to be so blunt, but that's pretty much what Jesus was saying to the man at the pool, wasn't it?

There is, by the way, nothing noble about hanging on to guilt when God says you are not guilty. It accomplishes nothing except wasting your time and energy.

There is nothing noble about looking God's word straight in the eye and denying that it applies to you because what you've done is too awful to be forgiven. Jesus said "It is finished" on the cross and He meant it – for you too!

Let me encourage you to take out a piece of paper and write on it all the things you have done in your life that you are holding against yourself – things you really feel guilty for. Once you have done that, write across that page or pages, "The blood of Jesus, God's Son, cleanses me from all sin." That's right out of 1 John 1:7 and applies to you because you are walking in the light with God about what you have done. Better yet, do this short exercise with somebody else with you that you trust.

Then do something radical with that list. Tear it up. Or, if it's safe to do so, burn it. Or bury it… and don't dig it up again. And make a declaration as you do so – something along the lines of:

> This is finally over. The blood of Jesus has cleansed me of all these sins (and more!), and I refuse to hold them against myself any longer. Since God forgives me, it is right to forgive myself because God's ways are perfect. I reject any and all accusations of the devil that would deceive me into thinking I am the exception to the rule. I fully accept my forgiveness in Christ. Thank You, Lord, that I am forgiven and free, innocent and not guilty in Christ... forever!

A THOUGHT TO CHEW ON

Since God says I am forgiven, I can and need to forgive myself.

A TRUTH TO REMEMBER

"The blood of Jesus His Son cleanses us from all sin" (1 John 1:7).

A QUESTION TO MULL OVER

If it is so clear in God's word that all who are in Christ are forgiven and not guilty (innocent), why is it that you struggle with forgiving yourself at times?

TALKING IT OVER WITH GOD

> *Dear Father, it seems like there is a real battle going on for my mind in this area of forgiveness. On the one hand, grasping hold of grace and letting go of this haunting guilt should be Christianity 101... basic stuff. And yet it's almost as if there is a restraining force that is trying to keep me (and, I suspect, many other followers of Jesus) from getting off the starting blocks and into the race.*

I suspect that is because there is something about knowing we're forgiven that is so freeing to people and therefore so threatening to the devil that he is bound and determined to try and dissuade us from believing we are truly not guilty in Christ. If I'm right in this suspicion, then more than ever I want to – no, I choose to – believe what You say about me.

I thank You that in Christ I am completely accepted, totally forgiven and unconditionally loved... whether my feelings agree with those statements or not. I choose to faith the facts even when those facts stand in direct opposition to my feelings. And I trust that those feelings will, in good time, obediently tag along for the ride. Amen.

Day 13: The Defense Rests

I remember the moment very distinctly. My wife, Shirley, and I were attending a conference that Dr Neil Anderson was presenting at the First Evangelical Free Church in Fullerton, California. That happened to be the church where the well-known Bible teacher, Dr Chuck Swindoll, was pastoring at the time. It was a huge auditorium and packed full with people.

Neil had just finished speaking on our identity in Christ and we happened to be sitting next to someone that we knew from our former ministry. Suddenly this friend of ours rose to her feet and said rather loudly, "That's a lie!"

Thinking back on that outburst, I'm glad she waited until the break rather than blurting that out during Neil's message! Anyway, Shirley and I turned quickly to look at her and I responded, "What's a lie?"

"I just had the thought that God is going to touch everyone's life in this room except mine."

"You're right," I replied. "That *is* a lie. God loves you as much as He loves anyone else in this place. And He is just as interested in working in your life as He is anybody else's life."

I'm glad Stacey (not her real name) had recognized that thought as a lie. The question is, where did it come from? After all, we were in a church and we were listening to good Bible teaching.

A number of years ago I was counseling a young man who was struggling with understanding God's grace and forgiveness. Jeremy (not his real name) had a problem with masturbation and not long before we met, a powerful thought came to his mind that if he masturbated one more time, God would leave him. As a result, Jeremy sincerely believed that God was fed up with him and if he messed up again, he would lose his salvation. Eventually he gave in to that temptation and had the horrible feeling that the Holy Spirit was exiting his life. He was understandably horrified.

What do these two instances have in common? They both involve God's sincere followers being attacked by thoughts from the accuser of the brethren (see Revelation 12:10). Satan's strategy of accusation is designed to persuade us to believe that we are less than who God says we are in Christ and that we are somehow unworthy to be loved or forgiven.

Stacey was under attack with thoughts that God didn't really love her, that she was the "exception to the rule" and that there was something inherently inferior about her that would cause God's blessings to pass her by.

Jeremy came under an enemy assault that sought to convince him he was denied the grace and forgiveness of God because of his sexual bondage. He came to believe that God was too holy and he (Jeremy) was too unholy for the Lord to forgive him and remain in his life. It was clear that the devil manufactured an experience that felt like the Holy Spirit leaving and that moment of deception further convinced Jeremy that he was doomed.

Maybe you have had an experience where the truth of God's word seemed drowned out by "doom and gloom" thoughts. Maybe you have been going through these devotionals and it seems like every time a scripture is presented that seems like it *should* give you hope and comfort, the negative thoughts swallow it up. And you still feel guilty.

One of the things we all need to realize is that there is no geographical location this side of heaven where we are completely safe from the enemy's attacks. Being in a church is no guarantee. Being at a great Bible-teaching conference does not grant automatic immunity. Even praying does not provide a fail-safe shield against the devil's strategies.

I'll let you know how the two stories ended in a minute, but before we go there, let's eavesdrop on a rather remarkable drama with an even more remarkable cast:

> Then he showed me Joshua the high priest standing before the angel of the LORD, and Satan standing at his right hand to accuse him. The LORD said to Satan, "The LORD rebuke you, Satan! Indeed, the LORD who has chosen Jerusalem rebuke you! Is this not a brand plucked from the fire?" Now Joshua was clothed with filthy garments and standing before the angel.
>
> Zechariah 3:1–3

This drama depicts a man of God (Joshua) who had committed some serious sin. We don't know what it is and we don't *need* know what it is. Whatever it was, Satan was all over it like a swarm of flies on garbage. You can almost hear him taunt, "You did *what*? Do you see how dirty and filthy he is, Lord? He must be punished! How can you even stand here in the presence of such holiness, Joshua? You have let the entire holy city of Jerusalem down. You're disgusting! You are not fit to be high priest!"

Like the most vicious prosecuting attorney, Satan can be relentless.

Notice something, though. Who defends him? That's right, the Lord. The Lord Himself tells Satan to shut up. And he does. He has to. Let's see how the story ends:

> He spoke and said to those who were standing before him, saying, "Remove the filthy garments from him." Again he said to him, "See, I have taken your iniquity away from you and will clothe you with festal robes."
>
> Zechariah 3:4

Sound familiar? That's right... putting on a new, clean robe was exactly what the father did with his younger son in the prodigal son story (Luke 15)! Just as the son was cleansed and restored, so too was Joshua in the Zechariah 3 story.

The angel of the Lord (who many believe was actually Jesus) took away Joshua's filthy garments, which were symbolic of his terrible sin, and he was then clothed once again with the righteous garments befitting a high priest. In fact he was even given a brand-spankin'-new, clean turban for his head, as the story goes on to tell us.

Maybe you can relate to Joshua. Because of the bad things you've done you feel as out of place with God as a man in dirty, sweaty workout clothes feels out of place at a great banquet filled with men in tuxedos and women in evening gowns.

But if you are in Christ you can say to Satan and all his accusations, "The Lord rebuke you, Satan! God has taken away my iniquity!" Then remind him of this scripture, speaking it with authority out loud:

> What then shall we say to these things? If God is for us, who is against us? He who did not spare His own Son, but delivered Him over for us all, how will He not also with Him freely give us all things? Who will bring a charge against God's elect? God is the one who justifies; who is the one who condemns?
>
> Romans 8:31–34a

You'll be happy to know that Stacey went on to fully enjoy the conference and the Lord did wonderful things in her life. She now knows that the Father's love for her is awesome (check out 1 John 3:1–3) and that she is not the exception to the rule.

As for Jeremy, he came to understand that God is gracious and would never leave him or forsake him (see Hebrews 13:5). So he renounced the accusation of the enemy that he was too unholy to stand before a holy God and declared that he was, in fact, the righteousness of God in Christ (2 Corinthians 5:21). He left our meeting with renewed hope and faith in the God of grace.

So there you have it. And your story can have an equally happy ending. When the prosecutor accuses you, remember that "if anyone sins, we have an Advocate [defense attorney] with the Father, Jesus Christ the righteous" (1 John 2:1). And Jesus has never lost a trial yet.

The defense rests.

A THOUGHT TO CHEW ON

The devil accuses us, trying to persuade us that we are less than the dearly loved, totally forgiven children of God we are.

A TRUTH TO REMEMBER

"If God is for us, who is against us?" (Romans 8:31).

A QUESTION TO MULL OVER

Why do you think the devil works so hard to make us disbelieve in God's gracious forgiveness of us in Christ?

TALKING IT OVER WITH GOD

Dear heavenly Father, thank You for exposing the devil's scheme of accusation. It makes me wonder how many times I have listened to his poisonous lies, thinking it was just me talking to myself or even God speaking with me. So many wasted hours of wallowing in miserable self-doubt and guilt. Thank You for forgiving me for not truly believing Your word.

I now choose to believe that what You say in the Bible is true, whether it feels true at that moment or not. Teach me how to tell when the devil is accusing me and lying to me. And make me so strong in You that standing firm against Satan and reminding him of what You say in Your word becomes second nature.

I thank You, Jesus, that You have never lost a court case to the evil prosecutor and You never will. I rest in Your defense. Amen.

Day 14: Should Your Conscience Be Your Guide?

A story in *Discipleship Journal* magazine has stuck with me ever since I read it a number of years ago. I can't help wondering how many of God's people feel this way. The article is entitled "I Don't Feel Like a Very Good Christian." Its subtitle is "Why does it seem that you can never quite measure up?" Here are a few excerpts:

> I could tell something was bothering my wife one evening – she was quieter than usual and didn't look at me as much. Finally, after the kids were put to bed, she said, "I don't know what's wrong." "What do you mean?" I asked. "Well," she said, "I don't... I just don't feel like a very good Christian."
>
> I wasn't sure what to say. I wanted to tell her that of course she was a wonderful Christian, but she didn't look like she was quite ready to believe that. So instead I asked, "What do you think is making you feel like that?" "I haven't had a quiet time for a while," she confessed. "After chasing two small kids all day, I feel wiped out; I'm too tired to read the Bible and pray. Mornings are crazy, and the kids don't nap at the same time, so I haven't had devotions in weeks. I'm not even sure I have a relationship with God anymore."

In this refreshingly transparent article, author Kevin Miller confessed that his wife wasn't the only one in the family struggling in this way:

> That week I had written in my journal, "Lord, I want to live more simply, as Jesus did, but I love money as much as anyone. I should be out ministering in some way, maybe at the nursing home, but I haven't got going.

I haven't been reading my Bible and praying like I should. And I want to lead family devotions on Sunday nights, but I've been so sporadic lately. I feel like I've failed you."[4]

You can't help but sympathize with this couple. They are clearly sincere Christian people who want to live in a way that pleases God. And it is most often not those who are lazy or spiritually unmotivated that suffer from this kind of guilt; it is those who genuinely desire to obey and serve Him.

So where are these guilt feelings coming from?

Most often, I believe, they come from a lack of understanding of God's grace. Is God so hard-hearted that He would be displeased with a mom who is working hard to responsibly care for her kids and happens to get worn out in the process? And is He so ungracious and exacting in His spiritual requirements of us that He would turn a blind eye to her faithful mothering and only be concerned that she hadn't had devotions?

I don't think so.

Now, it's clear that something needed to be adjusted in her life and schedule – maybe her husband or a friend or family member could chip in to help give her some breathers – but God was not the author of her feelings of guilt and condemnation. "Therefore there is now NO condemnation for those who are in Christ Jesus" (Romans 8:1, emphasis mine).

What then was the source of this guilt?

Chances are this dear lady was a victim of her own self-created value system. She had created her own idea of what a good Christian should do (likely thinking her own ideas reflected God's) and so her conscience was bothered since she was not measuring up. And so she felt guilty. Chances are the accuser of the brethren added his "amen" to all this false guilt as well.

Kevin's problems were similar. He had created a sort of "phantom" Christian husband and father – who was basically perfect – and that phantom haunted him because he was, like all of us, not perfect!

Notice the end result of Kevin's struggles? *I feel like I've failed you.* And his wife's conclusions went even deeper: *I'm not even sure I have a relationship with God anymore.* The end result of living (and failing!) under a self-imposed standard of righteousness is a guilty conscience, a sense of distance from God and, at times, despair.

Although Scripture tells us that we are to strive for a good conscience (1 Timothy 1:5) and that rejecting a clear conscience can be spiritually devastating (1 Timothy 1:19), the Bible also indicates that sometimes our hearts (reflected in our conscience) can simply be wrong:

> We will know by this that we are of the truth, and will assure our heart before Him in whatever our heart condemns us; for God is greater than our heart and knows all things.
>
> 1 John 3:19–20

Why would our heart (conscience) condemn us for something that God wouldn't? Simply because God is gracious and our conscience can often be programmed toward judging ourselves on a standard stricter than God's. For example, does God love us more if we have a quiet time, reading the Bible and praying? Certainly not, though He delights in spending time with us. But if we have somehow come to believe (even subconsciously) that having a daily quiet time ensures God's blessing on our lives and *not* having a quiet time puts us at risk of God withholding His blessing, then we will struggle with a falsely guilty conscience if we miss a day, or two, or three…

And the list of ways we falsely judge our worth or lovability with God can be almost endless: how we dress; how we wear our hair; what places we go or don't go; what kind of people we hang around with; the music we listen to; whether we read (or don't read) the Bible; how much we pray; which church we go to and how often we're there. And on and on. For some people there are so many rules and regulations to their life (none of which are in God's word) that the rules become their Ruler and laws become their Lord.

If that's what the Christian life is all about, count me out!

Is it any wonder that such people struggle with feelings of guilt, shame and fear (if they see themselves as performing poorly) or with a harsh, critical, judgmental, proud spirit (if they think they are doing well)? Do you really think Jesus would approve of such a system?

So what's the solution? How do you develop and protect a good and clear conscience while avoiding the false guilt of a conscience that makes one feel like a piece of dirt and that God is nearly impossible to please?

First, know that God is gracious and our acceptance and acceptability to Him has nothing to do with our performance. It has everything to do with Christ's performance and our putting our faith – lock, stock and barrel – in Christ. And when you realize that you are loved and accepted by God in Christ unconditionally, you actually *want to* and *enjoy* seeking and serving God out of a joyful, freed-up heart.

Second, realize that your conscience may need to go to school. If it has received its data on what is right and wrong from an increasingly immoral world system, your conscience will be too lenient and won't provide the "early warning system" it's supposed to by letting you know you are considering doing something that's bad. But if it has been educated by a rigid, legalistic family, church or cultural system, filled with rules and regulations that have never even entered the mind of God, then it is going to need to be retrained in the school of God's grace revealed in the Bible.

So, what answer would you give to the question posed by today's devotional title, "Should your conscience be your guide?" I would say a cautious "yes," let it be your guide. Just don't make it your God.

A THOUGHT TO CHEW ON

False guilt can feel like real guilt but can be the result of a poorly educated conscience.

A TRUTH TO REMEMBER

"Therefore there is now no condemnation for those who are in Christ Jesus" (Romans 8:1).

A QUESTION TO MULL OVER

Are you struggling with guilt feelings that are the result of an overly sensitive conscience? Have you added some man-made rules and regulations to your belief system that God does not have in His?

TALKING IT OVER WITH GOD

Dear heavenly Father, from what this devotional is saying, it sounds like my belief system – what I believe is right and wrong – may need anything from a little tune-up to a major overhaul. Thank You that it is not up to me to figure it all out.

First of all, in Christ I am truly forgiven and guilt is gone. I believe that, Lord, but help my unbelief! And that unbelief comes in the form of guilt feelings that plague me at times. When I feel guilty, would You please show me at that moment why I'm feeling that way? What are the ways in which I have allowed a counterfeit system of right and wrong to infiltrate my belief system and affect my heart? I want to renounce the rules, regulations, standards and expectations that breed false guilt and instead I want to respond only to the healthy, convicting work of the Holy Spirit.

Thank You that You know all things and are greater than my heart, and so You know when my heart is wrong and when it is telling the truth. I trust in You to be my God. Amen.

From Disgrace to Grace

Day 15: He's Got You Covered

It is very possible that even after going through last week's devotionals and rejoicing over your forgiveness in Christ, you may still sense that not all is right inside of you. It may be that there is something at the core of your being, deep down, that hasn't been touched, that still needs healing. It is possible that *guilt* is not your primary problem; instead you may be struggling with *shame*.

Guilt lets you know loud and clear that you have done something bad. *Shame*, on the other hand, sends the message that *you* are bad, that there is something inherently wrong with you as a person. Very often the shame-message that haunts us well into adulthood has its seeds planted early in life, in childhood, as this story illustrates:

> My dad was a very religious man who read the Bible for hours every day. He was an elder in our church and made sure our family was there every time the doors were open. But my dad's religion was often used as a rod of iron in our home.
>
> There were times when my dad would force me to pray and read the Bible aloud after disciplining me. I came to think of Bible reading as a form of punishment, and the regimented, forced prayer times convinced me that God was angry with me. If my mom and I were enjoying ourselves while watching an interesting program, my dad would get a scowl on his face and

turn off the TV. He would say, "Let's read the Bible." We were made to read Old Testament prophecy passages or genealogies with long, almost unpronounceable names.

I felt pressured and fearful, like I wasn't able to do anything right and that fun was wrong. Worse yet, I came to feel that *I* was wrong... like there was just something wrong with *me*. Adding to my shame was the fact that my dad could never truly believe I was saved. Countless times he would ask me if I was ready for Jesus' return. He would say, "You better be praying that you are worthy when Jesus comes back!"

One time a friend and I were reading Harlequin romance novels in my room, when my dad came in and grabbed them from us. With that awful scowl on his face, he tore the books apart page by page. Though there wasn't anything sexual about them, he acted like we were complete sluts for reading them. We were both crying. It was horrible.

His abuse was also verbal. When angry, my dad would say that I was lazy, that I was "a moron," and that I would never amount to anything. When I was a teenager, he would intently look at my face to examine my eye makeup. He would call me a "Jezebel" when he thought I was wearing too much. When he disapproved of my clothes, he would label me a "streetwalker."[5]

It is one thing to have your conduct criticized. It is quite another to have your character degraded and demeaned, like this poor lady. After all, if someone were to say that something you are doing is wrong and needs improving, at least you have some hope for change. You know what to focus on. By God's grace, you can stop smoking or swearing or lying or getting drunk or cheating people or... whatever it might be. It might be hard but the Bible assures us that you "can do all things through Him who strengthens" you (Philippians 4:13).

But when people attack your character and malign who you are, you feel defeated, deflated, defiled and despairing. You experience the "less mess" of feeling worth*less*, help*less*, meaning*less* and hope*less*. And that's no exaggeration. You can indeed come to the place of losing all hope.

And that is a crying shame.

This week we are going to study different facets of shame. We'll look at some of the reasons why we suffer from shame. We'll ask and try to answer the question of whether it is ever right to feel shame. We'll examine some of the ways we try and cope with shame on our own. And most importantly we'll seek to grasp God's absolutely brilliant antidote to shame.

Since this first devotional for the week is meant to introduce this crucial though painful topic, perhaps the following acronym might help you identify if shame is an issue for you. It describes some of the more common evidences of shame's presence in our lives. Do you ever find yourself experiencing the following things?

- **S**elf-consciousness or even self-hatred.
- **H**iding the real you or your past from people for fear of rejection.
- **A**nger at those who have contributed to your shame.
- **M**edicating your pain through drugs, alcohol, food, media diversions, etc.
- **E**xcelling in other areas to compensate for deep insecurities.

Did you know that shame and fear were the very first negative emotions felt by the human race? Prior to Adam and Eve eating from the tree of the knowledge of good and evil, they were described as "naked and... not ashamed" (Genesis 2:25). After their sin, they were naked and very ashamed and very fearful. Here's how the Bible describes this catastrophic change:

> Then the eyes of both of them were opened, and they knew that they were naked; and they sewed fig leaves together and made themselves loin coverings.
>
> They heard the sound of the LORD God walking in the garden in the cool of the day, and the man and his wife hid themselves from the presence of the LORD God among the trees of the garden.
>
> Genesis 3:7–8

Whereas in God's original creation, there was no shame associated with their physical bodies, sin instantly changed all that. Notice that Adam and Eve's first inclination was to cover up their private parts because of shame. Their second inclination was to try and hide themselves completely from God because of fear. Their first effort was sad; their second was just crazy. Trying to hide from God is like the little kid who covers his own eyes and then shouts triumphantly, "You can't see me!"

Because God is love, He sought out Adam and Eve and had a talk with them. Because God is also just, He proclaimed His judgment upon man, woman, the ground, childbirth and even the snake (Satan). This whole scene is a tragedy, as they say, of biblical proportions and opened up a Pandora's box of all manner of evils on the human race and planet earth, from which we are still reeling today.

But in the midst of the judgment and sadness and loss and pain, don't miss the grace of God. In this tragedy, there is the foreshadowing of a final solution to shame that would one day come through the One whose heel would be bruised as He crushed the serpent's head (Genesis 3:15). That One would be Jesus Himself, our Deliverer from Shame.

This foreshadowing should bring great hope to you today, knowing that the God who "heals the brokenhearted and binds up their wounds" (Psalm 147:3) saw Adam and Eve's shame and He sees yours. And He knew, and He knows, just what to do to alleviate their suffering and yours:

> The LORD God made garments of skin for Adam and his wife, and clothed them.
>
> Genesis 3:21

That may not seem like much, but it was. It was the first time a living creature had been killed. Death was not supposed to be part of life on earth and it didn't even exist until Adam and Eve sinned. But the foreshadowing of the shed blood of the Lamb of God (Jesus), who takes away the sin and shame of the world, came through the sacrifice of an animal whose skin became the covering over the sin and shame of the first humans.

And this same God who came to the rescue when Adam and Eve sinned will come to your rescue, too. He's got you covered.

A THOUGHT TO CHEW ON

Guilt means we have done something wrong. Shame makes us feel like *we* are what is wrong.

A TRUTH TO REMEMBER

"The LORD God made garments of skin for Adam and his wife, and clothed them" (Genesis 3:21).

A QUESTION TO MULL OVER

Which aspects of the SHAME acronym do you see at work most in your life? Are these coping mechanisms really working for you?

TALKING IT OVER WITH GOD

Dear heavenly Father, it is powerfully clear from Your word that sin rocked the human race to the core... instantly. And it has affected the entire world, not just humankind. It makes me stop in my tracks to acknowledge how futile it was for Adam and Eve to try and cover it all up and hide when the fabric of life was ripped to shreds and the foundation of the planet unalterably cracked at that moment. And it also brings me face to face with the utter futility of me thinking there is anything I can do in my own strength to cover up or hide from sin's effects in my life.

Thank You that I know the end of the story – what You did through Jesus to heal my broken heart and bind up my wounds. This week, Lord, I welcome You into the covered-up and hidden places of my soul so that You can remove my shame and restore me to unashamed joy with Your clean garments of righteousness. Amen.

Day 16: A Second Chance

Why do we feel shame? One of the reasons we feel shame is as a result of the wrong things we have done. This kind of shame can land us anywhere on a continuum from mild embarrassment (the low end of the spectrum) to deep humiliation and being ostracized by society (the high end).

Shame from what we have done wrong intensifies in proportion to the depth of the "badness" of our deeds (according to our personal and societal standards), the breadth of public exposure of our misdeeds, and the length of time we are negatively in the public eye.

An individual might feel a certain measure of shame for being caught by the police for driving while under the influence of alcohol. But if that DUI is committed by someone in local political office and the story is picked up by the local newspaper and TV newscast, the shame would increase. Add to that the tragedy of someone being killed by that drunk driver, with the consequent well-publicized trial and eventual imprisonment, and you have an even greater potential for deep, long-term shame.

You get the picture.

Should we feel shame? Is it ever an appropriate emotion? If someone were to scold us and point a finger at us and say, "You should be ashamed of yourself!", is that ever a valid rebuke? Those are really good questions. We'll try and answer them in a minute, but first a brief bit of time travel back to 1974.

I remember the incident all too well. I was twenty years old and a junior (third-year university) meteorology student taking a weather forecasting class. I was well liked and highly respected by the professor and my classmates. Riding the crest of that popularity and success, I volunteered to be the first student to do a "map discussion" (an analysis of that day's major weather trends) of the United States.

Those were the days when we had to draw our own weather maps and make forecasts based on weather station observations and early computer forecasting models. Pretty primitive by today's standards. I was given two and a half hours to go up to the weather station, do my analysis, draw the weather maps, and prepare the discussion to present to the class and the professor.

I was pumped. I thought it would be a breeze. But never have 150 minutes of time passed so quickly! I could feel my anxiety and blood pressure levels rising as the minutes rocketed by. Finally, my prep time was up. I didn't feel prepared at all, but it was time to step up to the plate... ready or not!

To say I struck out would be an understatement.

Almost immediately the professor started poking holes in my analysis. He pointed out things that I should have taken into account but had overlooked. After about ten to fifteen minutes of humiliation the professor pretty much ignored me (though I was still standing up front) and asked the rest of the class questions about the forecast. Of course, all their answers were right. A few were so haughty about it that I believe strangling them at that moment would have been considered justifiable homicide.

I felt like a complete idiot.

I remember walking out of that class totally defeated. I had failed miserably in my first "test" as a forecaster in my chosen career field. I wanted to crawl into a hole. I could tell the professor – who was highly respected in the field – was deeply disappointed, almost disgusted, with me. My classmates reveled in their ascension to honor in the professor's eyes and my plummeting into dishonor. I had one friend who tried to console me, but I was inconsolable. I thought about quitting and changing my major.

The shame was almost unbearable.

Now, I had obviously not committed a crime, but though crime wasn't involved, sin was – the sin of pride and arrogance. I'm talking here about mine. So the Lord orchestrated a "fall" for me, as His word promises (Proverbs 16:18). Was shame in this instance a legitimate emotion for me to feel?

Maybe this chunk of Scripture from one of the apostle Paul's writings will shed some light on the place of shame in the life of a follower of Christ:

> Does any one of you, when he has a case against his neighbor, dare to go to law before the unrighteous and not before the saints? Or do you not know that the saints will judge the world? If the world is judged by you, are you not competent to constitute the smallest law courts? Do you not know that we will judge angels? How much more matters of this life? So if you have law courts dealing with matters of this life, do you appoint them as judges who are of no account in the church? I say this to your shame. Is it so, that there is not among you one wise man who will be able to decide between his brethren, but brother goes to law with brother, and that before unbelievers?
>
> 1 Corinthians 6:1–6

It's pretty obvious Paul was ticked off. He fired off seven questions in order to point out their shame. The apostle couldn't believe what was going on. Believers were suing one another in courts run by unbelievers! Paul reminded the saints they were going to judge the world and even angels one day, so why would they allow themselves to be judged by the very ones they would one day judge? It didn't make sense.

Reading between the lines, the "shame" that Paul was pointing out was that God's people were not living up to who they were in Christ. They had the wisdom to handle disputes themselves but they were being a terrible witness for Christ by airing all their dirty laundry in secular courts instead. Later in that chapter Paul practically moaned at them, saying that it would have been better if everybody had just suffered the financial loss rather than parading their lack of love for each other before unbelievers.

They should have known better. And they were right to feel shame, if indeed any of them did. Any time we engage in behavior that is contrary to who we are in Christ, we are right to feel badly about ourselves.

So the key issue for followers of Christ is not to deny our shameful deeds and hide our sins or pretend that we are fine when we're not. Nor is it right or smart to wallow in our shame either. The key to dealing with our shame from the wrong things we have done is found in 2 Corinthians 4:1–2:

> Therefore, since we have this ministry, as we received mercy, we do not lose heart, but we have renounced the things hidden because of shame, not walking in craftiness or adulterating the word of God, but by the manifestation of truth commending ourselves to every man's conscience in the sight of God.

It is easy to lose heart and feel really down and defeated when we mess up. We must remember that we have already received the mercy of God in Christ and that we are forgiven. Some people, however, do not receive God's mercy and foolishly choose to continue hiding their sin because of the shame they feel. Some end up becoming really clever at tricking others into thinking they are walking in purity when they are not. Others even go so far as declaring that the Bible doesn't actually call the sinful deeds they are doing sin! You really don't want to go down that road.

So when you sin, own up to it. Don't try to hide. Receive God's merciful cleansing and forgiveness and renounce (declare your total rejection of) that sin and keep on walking.

And know that God is a God of second chances... and third... and fourth... and...

Speaking of second chances, because I was brave enough to be the first one to do a map discussion, my professor ended up cutting me a lot of slack. So I didn't quit and decide to major in basket weaving or something. I actually got a second chance to do a map discussion toward the end of the term and it couldn't have gone better. The professor was thrilled. I got an "A" for the course. And God humbled a proud student, allowing him to suffer shame but not stay there. That's grace.

A THOUGHT TO CHEW ON

Shame comes when we live below the level of who we are as a saint, a child of God.

A TRUTH TO REMEMBER

"... we have renounced the things hidden because of shame" (2 Corinthians 4:2).

A QUESTION TO MULL OVER

Are there things that you are hiding because of shame? Are there any ways you are trying to trick people into thinking you are more righteous than you actually are? Are you growing to doubt some of the things the Bible says are clearly wrong in order to avoid admitting your sin and facing your shame?

TALKING IT OVER WITH GOD

Dear heavenly Father, I thank You that You are a God of second chances and far more than that. I guess I have a choice: I can either hide and try to cover up things I do wrong out of the shame of not being as good as I should be or out of the fear of disapproval or rejection, or I can renounce the things hidden because of shame. The first choice is the path to deeper slavery to sin and shame. The second is the road to freedom.

I thank You for forgiving me for the many times I have lived life at a level far below that which is fitting for a saint, a child of God. I choose not to wallow in the shame of my failure, but instead receive Your mercy and my full cleansing in Christ, as well as Your power to live life in a way that is worthy of my calling in Christ.

I will lift my head up high today – not in pride, but in full recognition of who I am in You: part of a royal priesthood, a holy nation, a people that belong to You, so that I might proclaim Your excellencies as You have called me out of the darkness of sin and shame into Your marvelous light (1 Peter 2:9–10)! Amen.

Day 17: A Return to Dignity

In addition to experiencing shame from what we have done, we can also experience shame from what others have done to us. The capacity for man's inhumanity to man is almost unfathomable and the enemy of our souls takes a perverse delight in enslaving humankind with the shame that comes from abuse.

But in Christ there can be a heroic return to dignity even in the face of the worst degradation. The following story, though not "Christian" per se, suggests some powerful spiritual parallels that should bring you hope if shame is your shadow or if it dogs the steps of someone you love:

> During World War Two, American Lieutenant General Jonathan Mayhew Wainwright was commander of the Allied Forces in the Philippines. Following a heroic resistance against enemy forces, he was forced to surrender the island of Corregidor on May 6, 1942. He, along with many others, was taken captive by the Japanese.
>
> For three years he suffered terribly as a prisoner of war in a camp in Manchuria, China. During that time he endured a constant barrage of almost unbelievable cruelty – malnutrition, physical and emotional abuse, and relentless psychological mind-games.
>
> Throughout the three years of imprisonment, Wainwright somehow maintained his dignity as a human being and soldier. But incredibly, even after the Japanese surrendered to end World War Two, his captors kept him and the other American prisoners behind bars! The war was over, but their bondage continued.
>
> One day an Allied plane landed in a field near the prison, and through the fence that surrounded the compound, an airman informed the general of the news: *Japan had surrendered. The Allies had won!*

Wainwright immediately pulled his frail and emaciated body to attention, then turned and marched toward the Japanese command house. He burst through the door and strode up to the camp's commanding officer.

"My Commander-in-Chief has conquered your Commander-in-Chief. I am now in charge of this camp," Wainwright declared.

In response, the Japanese officer took off his sword, laid it on the table, and surrendered his command.[6]

Wow! Kind of makes you want to cheer, doesn't it? Or at least cheer up.

The good news is that though we can feel terrible shame for the things people have done to us, there are some things they can never take away. And one of them is our dignity. The Bible says that all people – Christians or not – have been created in the image of God (Genesis 1:27). I don't think any of us fully understands what this means, but it's clear that we are the apple of God's eye, the crowning glory of His creation; that He has given us freedom to choose, the ability to plan, to dream, to create; and He has made us with the capacity for wisdom, for love, for grace, for justice, and to have an intimate relationship with God Himself.

And even though that image of God has been tarnished and fractured through sin, it is still there and no amount of abuse of our physical bodies or twisting of our minds can fully obscure the image of God in us.

But there is much more shame-defeating dignity for us who are in Christ, and that is where the parallels to today's story come in.

The shame and humiliation heaped on Lieutenant General Wainwright and his men was very real. I'm sure the degradation they experienced became a source of great amusement and derision to their captors. But shame need not penetrate our souls. The general maintained his dignity as a human being and soldier through all he suffered, because nobody can take that dignity from us; it can only be surrendered by us. In the same way, no matter what is done to us, and no matter how shamefully people treat us, no one can touch our core identity – who we are in Christ. And out of our *identity in Christ* powerfully flows our *authority in Christ*. And indeed our Commander-in-Chief, the Lord Jesus Christ, has conquered our enemies' commander-in-chief, Satan. And when we stand in our authority in Christ, the devil must stand down.

And so, though it is understandable that we experience shame when we are treated shamefully, there is a way that will enable us to rise above debilitating shame. It is the way of truth, the truth of who we *really* are in God's eyes... regardless of what people might say or think or do. To help you experience the dignity of your untouchable, incorruptible identity in Christ, I encourage you to make the following declarations out loud if you have suffered shame in these areas (and if you haven't, take a few minutes to express your gratitude to God and to pray for those you know who have suffered):

Sexual abuse, rape or exploitation

I renounce the lie that I am dirty or my body is dirty because of the sexual acts perpetrated on me. I am not a slut, whore, prostitute, sex slave, or [fill in any other names you might have been called or called yourself]. *I have been made clean by the word Jesus has spoken to me (John 15:3). I am not trash and my body is not just somebody's plaything. My body is the temple of the Holy Spirit, Who is in me and will never leave me or forsake me. I have been bought with a price, the precious blood of Jesus (1 Corinthians 6:19–20;*

Hebrews 13:5; 1 Peter 1:18–19). And I renounce the lie that I am a victim, but I announce that in Christ I am a victor, more than a conqueror through Him who loved me (Romans 8:37). And I refuse to become like those who have done these things to me, so I reject hate and choose forgiveness in Christ (Ephesians 4:31–32).

Emotional and demeaning verbal abuse

I renounce the lie that I am dumb, stupid, a moron; that I can't do anything right; that it would have been better if I had never been born; that I am unloved, unwanted and that I don't belong or [fill in any other name or practice that demeaned you]. *I renounce all the disgusted looks, raised and harsh voices, sarcastic remarks, cutting jokes, nasty and derisive comments, favoritism to others, neglect of my basic needs for love, affection and security. I declare that how I have been treated says much more about the character of my abusers than it does about me. I announce that in Christ the Lord my God in my midst is mighty. He will sing and rejoice over me with joy. He will quiet me in His love and shout with joy over me (Zephaniah 3:17). The Lord delights in me (Isaiah 62:4) and He takes pleasure in me (Psalm 149:4). I am the apple of His eye (Zechariah 2:8), and so not only am I precious to Him but He will protect and shield me.*

As I was writing today's devotional, a very clear message from the Lord filled my heart. I want to tell you something that I pray and hope you'll never forget:

Who you are is who GOD (and no one else!) says you are.

In Christ, shame is defeated. Dignity is restored. And the journey to return to dignity begins with the heart of faith that says, *Yes, Lord, I believe You.* Won't you begin that journey today?

For I am the LORD your God, who upholds your right
    hand,
Who says to you, "Do not fear, I will help you."

Isaiah 41:13

A THOUGHT TO CHEW ON

Who you are is who *God* (and no one else!) says you are.

A TRUTH TO REMEMBER

"… the LORD delights in you" (Isaiah 62:4).

A QUESTION TO MULL OVER

What demeaning or degrading name(s) still clings to your
soul that you need to renounce? How does God see you?

TALKING IT OVER WITH GOD

*Dear heavenly Father, sometimes it seems like the whole
world is throwing lies at me that are aimed right at my
heart, and You are the only One telling me the truth. I
really need Your help in guarding my heart so that the
shame that wants to swallow me whole is evicted from my
soul. I thank You that Your word is living and active and
sharper than any two-edged sword and that it pierces to
the very division of my soul and my spirit. Therefore it
can shred the enemy's lies and implant truth at the deepest
level of my heart.*

*I choose today to renounce all the lies that have caused
me shame* [go ahead and name them specifically] *and I
choose to believe the truth of who You say that I am. I will
take this first step in my journey to return to dignity in
You. And I thank You that You will hold my right hand all
the way. Amen.*

Day 18: Let Love In

I have this friend, Rock, who preached a sermon at our church a while back, and he said some pretty rock-solid things about shame and love. Rock, by the way, played college football and has been a pastor. I think his name really fits a tough and tender man of God. "Rock." Pretty cool. My name, Rich, would be very appropriate for a football player to have, but probably not that cool for a pastor. Anyway, here's what Rock said:

> The shame messages from our past can rob us of the love messages God has for us in the present. Where you have been unloved, you are emotionally wounded. The shame and lack of experience of God's love in those places can feel so true, and so we come to believe at some level that we are unlovable.

And then he asked the question:

> Will you let God into those unloved, ashamed places?

Rock on!

There is a story from the life of King David that may connect with how you feel. Even more importantly, I hope it helps you connect with how God feels about you. The story begins with David asking his servants a question:

> Is there yet anyone left of the house of Saul, that I may show him kindness for Jonathan's sake?
>
> 2 Samuel 9:1

In case your Old Testament history is a bit rusty, Saul reigned as king before David and Jonathan was Saul's son. Saul had chased David around the countryside, trying to kill him numerous times. The fact that David wanted to show kindness to one of Saul's relatives is a bit surprising, to say the least. God amazingly shows grace to His enemies!

Jonathan and David, on the other hand, were best friends. Each had pledged, should either of them die, to take care of the surviving members of the dead one's family. In a terrible battle against the Philistines, both Saul and Jonathan had been killed on Mount Gilboa, and a while later David had remembered his covenant with Jonathan and so was wondering if there was anyone left to help. It turns out there was:

> And Ziba said to the king, "There is still a son of
> Jonathan who is crippled in both feet."
>
> 2 Samuel 9:3

Though this son of Jonathan was now apparently an adult, when he was five years old he tripped and injured himself while his nurse was hurrying him to safety, resulting in the damage to his feet. The lame man's name was Mephibosheth (2 Samuel 4:4), which sounds a bit like something you might yell out when you accidentally hit your thumb with a hammer.

Anyway, Ziba brings "Mef" to David at the king's request. Let's pick up the story back in 2 Samuel 9:6–8:

> Mephibosheth, the son of Jonathan the son of Saul, came
> to David and fell on his face and prostrated himself.
> And David said, "Mephibosheth." And he said, "Here is
> your servant!" David said to him, "Do not fear, for I will
> surely show kindness to you for the sake of your father
> Jonathan, and will restore to you all the land of your
> grandfather Saul; and you shall eat at my table regularly."
> Again he prostrated himself and said, "What is your
> servant, that you should regard a dead dog like me?"

This is really a great story. "Mef" was terrified that David was going to kill him, probably figuring David wanted to make darn sure there was no chance a descendant of Saul would one day lay claim to the throne. That was a valid fear. Kings tended to do those kinds of things in those days.

But David did the exact opposite. He restored to "Mef" honor, dignity and land so that he would be a "rich rock" in the community. In fact, later in the story, King David commanded Ziba and his fifteen sons and twenty servants to farm "Mef's" land so that he'd always have plenty to eat (verse 10). Here's the happy ending:

> So Mephibosheth ate at David's table as one of the king's sons. Mephibosheth had a young son whose name was Mica. And all who lived in the house of Ziba were servants to Mephibosheth. So Mephibosheth lived in Jerusalem, for he ate at the king's table regularly. Now he was lame in both feet.

> 2 Samuel 9:11b–13

In today's society we have learned how to make life a little bit easier for those who are disabled (special restrooms, ramps, parking spaces, etc.), but in the days of the Old Testament, being blind, lame, disfigured, deformed or otherwise defective was viewed as a curse. It prohibited someone from serving as a priest (Leviticus 21:16–21) and was a source of great shame. No wonder "Mef" thought of himself as a "dead dog."

I think that's why the story ends with the statement, "Now he was lame in both feet." To treat a lame man like David did was an act of unprecedented kindness and grace.

Now, you may not be lame, and you likely would not refer to yourself as a "dead dog" – at least, maybe not with those exact words. But you may be able to relate to "Mef" a lot, and would have shared his astonishment at being treated kindly and graciously by anyone, especially by the king. Maybe you, like Rock said earlier, have some places that are unloved... and so you have come to view yourself, at some level, as *unlovable*.

Every one of us needs to have someone in our lives who believes in us, who knows we have worth and who is committed to helping us be all we were created to be. In the midst of the grossest days of my teenage acne, skeletal skinniness, bad breath and worse personality, I had an English teacher who liked me and believed in my writing. True, she was a bit quirky (and not just because she liked me!), as she demonstrated by having us spend about half the year analyzing Simon and Garfunkel's song, "The Sound of Silence," but by her encouragement I submitted something I wrote to a teen magazine and got it published! That meant a lot to me.

Mephibosheth had King David. I had Ms Garfunkel (not her real name). Who do you have? Who is there in your life that looks at the shame of what you've done and who others say you are and says, "I believe in you anyway"?

In case you didn't realize it, Jesus is a firm believer in you. Through Him and in Him, God *redefines* you. The apostle Paul talks about that in 2 Corinthians 5:16–18a:

> Therefore from now on we recognize no one according to the flesh; even though we have known Christ according to the flesh, yet now we know Him in this way no longer. Therefore if anyone is in Christ, he is a new creature; the old things passed away; behold, new things have come. Now all these things are from God, who reconciled us to Himself through Christ and gave us the ministry of reconciliation...

Summary? God doesn't judge a book by its cover, and neither should we. It's the story inside that counts, and in Christ God has written a whole new novel about our lives and it has a very happy ending. And God wants us now to be an open book for others to read so that they can meet the Author and have their story rewritten, too.

I love this verse, 1 John 4:16:

> We have come to know and have believed the love which God has for us. God is love, and the one who abides in love abides in God, and God abides in him.

Probably you know (at least in your head) that God loves you. Could it be that it's time you finally came to *believe* it?

A THOUGHT TO CHEW ON

We all need someone in our lives who believes in us.

A TRUTH TO REMEMBER

"We have come to know and have believed the love which God has for us" (1 John 4:16a).

A QUESTION TO MULL OVER

"Mef" thought of himself as a "dead dog." How do you view yourself? What does 2 Corinthians 5:16–18 have to say about the name(s) you call yourself or others call you?

TALKING IT OVER WITH GOD

Dear heavenly Father, it's natural, isn't it, to try and protect myself? If I have a cut, I put a Band-Aid on it. If I break a bone, the doc puts a cast on it. Knee braces, slings, gauze bandages, and all that stuff are designed to protect wounded and injured places from a dirty world and give them a chance to heal.

In my soul I have wounds and I have tried to hide those places from the curious and not-always-gracious eyes of those around me. In so doing I have hoped that I would forget those places are there, too, and that maybe, somehow they would heal. But the wounds haven't healed, have they?

As I said earlier, it is the "natural" thing to do. But Your word says that the natural man does not accept the things of the Spirit of God (1 Corinthians 2:14a). So, what I'm needing, Lord, is not a "natural" way of coping with my shame, but a "supernatural" path to healing. And that can only come through You.

Knowing and believing the love You have for me, I choose to open the locked doors and hidden closets of my life to Your love, because You indeed are love. Thank You for believing in me and for Your grace that covers and removes my shame. Amen.

Day 19: Adopted and Accepted

The memory of that moment is forever etched in my mind, having been captured on my video camera back in 1999. Our newly adopted Thai son, Lua Saibua, was walking slowly down the sidewalk of the Rangsit Babies' Home, hand in hand with our oldest daughter, Michelle, who was eight years old at the time. A few minutes later our whole family piled into a minivan with the translators and we headed to our hotel in Bangkok. Lua never looked back. Life at the orphanage was over; life as a Miller had begun. About ten months later his adoption was finalized in the Superior Court of the County of Gwinnett outside of Atlanta, Georgia.

It amazes me when I think about all that transpired in Lua's life during those days. He became a citizen of a new country; he had new parents; he had a new brother and new sisters and a new extended family; he wore new clothes and played with new toys; he had a new place to live; he had to learn a new language, adjust to a new climate, get used to new buildings, plants, animals, faces and food; he entered a new school and became part of a church for the first time in his life.

It would have been overwhelming for most people, but Lua never seemed overwhelmed. He just kind of went with the flow… except when he couldn't get his way. Then all you-know-what would break loose. As we learned, it is one thing to get the boy out of the orphanage; it's quite another to get the orphanage out of the boy!

You might wonder how Shirley and I knew the Lord wanted us to adopt. There were a lot of factors, not the least of which was a growing yearning in our hearts to do so. But the confirmation came one day through Matthew 18:12–14:

> What do you think? If any man has a hundred sheep, and one of them has gone astray, does he not leave the ninety-nine on the mountains and go and search for the one that is straying? If it turns out that he finds it, truly I say to you, he rejoices over it more than over the ninety-nine which have not gone astray. So it is not the will of your Father who is in heaven that one of these little ones perish.

God told me clearly, "Go after the one." And so we did. It was not the will of our Father that four-year-old Lua perish.

Did you know that you are an adopted child, that it is not the will of our Father that you perish either (see 2 Peter 3:9)? Well, it's true. If you belong to Christ, you are adopted into His family. You are a citizen of a new country (Philippians 3:20), with a new Father, new brothers and sisters, a new language (called *faith*), and a new church (the global body of Christ). You've even been given a new heart and a new spirit (Ezekiel 36:26). You literally have a new life – the life of Christ in you (1 John 5:11–13).

Maybe you didn't know that you were adopted. I'm not sure Lua had any idea what was going on when we whisked him off from Thailand to America. The term "adoption" would have been meaningless to him, though it was most certainly happening to him. And since Lua is a special needs child, we're still not sure how much he understands. But here's what the "Final Judgment and Decree of Adoption" for Lua Saibua says:

> IT IS HEREBY ORDERED, ADJUDGED, and DECREED that the Petition for Adoption is granted and that this Final Judgment and Decree of Adoption be entered. The Court hereby terminates all the rights of the biological parents to said child, and the Court hereby declares the child to be the adopted child of the Petitioners, capable

of inheriting their respective estates according to law...
The relationship between Shirley Grace Miller and the
child, and Richard Edward Miller and the child, as to
their legal rights and liabilities, shall be the relationship
of parent and child, as provided by law.

That's exactly what happened to you when you became a child
of God! All rights of ownership of the evil one toward you
were terminated. You were transferred, moved, smuggled out
of the domain of darkness and brought into the kingdom of
God's Son (Colossians 1:13). Look what God has to say about
your adoption:

For all who are being led by the Spirit of God, these
are sons of God. For you have not received a spirit of
slavery leading to fear again, but you have received a
spirit of adoption as sons by which we cry out, "Abba!
Father!" The Spirit Himself testifies with our spirit that
we are children of God, and if children, heirs also, heirs
of God and fellow heirs with Christ, if indeed we suffer
with Him so that we may also be glorified with Him.

Romans 8:14–17

Sometimes shame makes us think we don't belong. And
maybe you have felt like you never fit in, that others didn't
want you, that you were an outsider, a misfit. An orphan.

God wants you to know that we have been welcomed
into His family, on an equal footing with all other followers
of Christ around the world, with an incredible inheritance
waiting in heaven for us (see 1 Peter 1:3–5).

You do belong. You have been accepted in the Beloved
[Christ] by God's grace (Ephesians 1:6). The Bible also says
that we are to warmly welcome each other, just like God
warmly welcomed us:

Therefore, accept one another, just as Christ also
accepted us to the glory of God.

Romans 15:7

I think it is possible to know we are *loved* but still not believe
we are *accepted*. Have you ever thought about that? We may
know that God chose us and sincerely cares about us, but we
believe that somehow we need to clean up our act or improve
our performance in order to fully "make the team." Only then
will we be acceptable and accepted, or so we think.

Adoption settles the issue once and for all. When you
adopt a kid, all kinds of baggage come along for the ride. That
was sure the case with Lua. He has major anger issues; has
ADHD; learns at an extremely slow rate; is pretty insecure (he
still sucks his thumb at age seventeen); and makes the same
mistakes over and over again.

Hmmm, sounds a lot like the rest of us, doesn't it... minus
maybe the thumb sucking!

But we cannot imagine our family without him. I would
die for him, as would the rest of the family, and he is as much
a Miller as our three biological, higher-achieving kids.

God cannot imagine His family without you. He would
die for you... in fact, He already did. And you are as much a
part of the family of God as the Christian superstars you hear
about and respect. God is not waiting for you to "improve"
before He puts out the welcome mat for you. You're already
on the team, in the family, in the game, and your Father is
excited about all the "goals" you will score in your life!

And, by the way, there's one more thing new about Lua
that I failed to mention... his name. His new name is Luke.

Adopted and accepted. That's you. God is not ashamed
of you and Jesus is not ashamed to call you brother or sister
(see Hebrews 2:11). So why are you ashamed?

And you've been given a new name, too. Stay tuned for that story tomorrow.

A THOUGHT TO CHEW ON

In Christ we have been fully adopted and completely accepted into God's family. God is not ashamed of me.

A TRUTH TO REMEMBER

"For you have not received a spirit of slavery leading to fear again, but you have received a spirit of adoption as sons by which we cry out, 'Abba! Father!'" (Romans 8:15).

A QUESTION TO MULL OVER

What does it mean to be "accepted" by God? Try and come up with some words or phrases from everyday life that would be really meaningful for you in grasping this truth about your relationship with God.

TALKING IT OVER WITH GOD

Abba! Father! I can really come to You, calling on You with those names, can't I? Daddy! Father! I think about how earthly dads' hearts are so warmed when their kids run to them, calling them "Daddy!", and it wouldn't surprise me if Your heart is warmed, too. Thank You for adopting me into Your family and making me feel so welcome. It is really true that You are not ashamed to call me Your child and that Jesus is not ashamed to be my big brother.

I can see how at times I am fully convinced of Your love for the world, as in John 3:16, and there are even times I'm sure of Your personal, one-on-one love for me. But probably more times than not I have the nagging doubt that You don't really accept me as I am right now... that

You sort of tolerate me but would be a lot happier if I were more like somebody else.

Please forgive me, Father, for doubting Your acceptance of me and for thinking I had to do something to make myself acceptable to You. Your Son did that already, didn't He? What amazing grace! Amen.

Day 20: A New Name

I was attending a two-week Practicum which was one of the requirements of the Master's degree in Christian counseling that I was pursuing. One day we heard a speaker who encouraged us to ask God to show us what our "old name" and "new name" were. By "old name" he was referring to that label that we had worn on our soul, perhaps most of our lives, that haunted us and dogged our steps, even after we had experienced new life in Christ. By "new name" he wasn't talking about trying to get a sneak peek at the new name written on the white stone that Jesus said we'd get in heaven (Revelation 2:17). He meant a name, title or phrase that was particularly meaningful to us and that connected our hearts with our new identity in Christ.

Most of us can readily identify the "old names." Things like "stupid," "jerk," "fat," "klutz," "can't do anything right," "wish you'd never been born," "dirty," "getting what you deserve" and so on can be vivid, constant reminders of past failures, rejection and abuse. Some "old names," on the other hand, can seem helpful, like "star," "strong one," "can do anything you put your mind to," "leader," "in charge," "everybody's counting on you" and so on, while actually they serve as a lead weight around our necks, burdening us and even crushing us with a load of responsibility beyond our ability or maturity.

Aside from a few stories from college, I haven't really given you much information about my growing-up years. Not that there's anything particularly earth-shaking to talk about, but a few comments here might put my journey to discover both my "old name" and "new name" into a helpful context.

After a reasonably enjoyable childhood, about age 11, puberty hit. I thought it was a terminal illness. In one year I

went from 5 foot 6 inches and 120 pounds to 6 foot 2 inches…
and 120 pounds. I wasn't skinny; I was skeletal. To make
matters worse, acne broke out on my face and elsewhere. I
also had braces on my teeth like a lot of kids, but I didn't do a
very good job of keeping them clean. OK, have I grossed you
out yet? We'll take a break here for you to gag.

All right, back to the story. As you know, pre-teen and
early-teen kids are insecure, to say the least. Because of that
insecurity, they often search desperately for someone at school
that they view as worse off than they are. That poor person
then becomes a target for ridicule. It makes the critic feel a
bit better and shifts the spotlight off his or her imperfections
and onto the chosen victim. Care to guess who got "hired"
for that job?

To be honest, the rejection and humiliation I went through
for a few years were really painful. I was always afraid that
nobody would let me sit near them in the lunchroom, so I
often would find a vacant classroom to eat alone, bringing a
sack lunch from home. I was lonely and angry and sad and
hateful. If I ever wanted someone to play with, I had to call
them up and try and get them to come over to spend time
with me. There were a couple of kids who would actually do
that, which kept me from going completely loony.

When I took the Practicum speaker's advice and asked
the Lord to show me my "old name," it took about two days
before the perfect description hit me. It was "outcast." That's
exactly how I felt and even long after finding new life in
Christ, I would at times feel like nobody wanted me around.
There was still a tremendous amount of shame in my soul.

What about my "new name"? Well, the first thing to
recognize is that God is into giving out new names. In the
Bible, Jacob became Israel. Simon became Peter. Saul became
Paul. And new names are extremely important to God, as

they are indicative of a change of heart, a change of identity, a change of character. Even Israel itself is promised a new name in Isaiah 62:2–5, indicative of a new relationship with her God:

> The nations will see your righteousness,
> And all kings your glory;
> And you will be called by a new name
> Which the mouth of the LORD will designate.
> You will also be a crown of beauty in the hand of the
>   LORD,
> And a royal diadem in the hand of your God.
> It will no longer be said to you, "Forsaken,"
> Nor to your land will it any longer be said, "Desolate";
> But you will be called, "My delight is in her,"
> And your land, "Married";
> For the LORD delights in you,
> And to Him your land will be married.
> For as a young man marries a virgin,
> So your sons will marry you;
> And as the bridegroom rejoices over the bride,
> So your God will rejoice over you.

Since the Church, the body of Christ, is also one day to be the bride of Christ (see 2 Corinthians 11:2; Revelation 19:7–8), I have no problem seeing that followers of the Lord Jesus are somehow the graced beneficiaries of these beautiful promises as well, including a "new name." It would be a great idea for you to take a few minutes and think about the Lord's great love for you expressed in that Isaiah passage above.

As for my "new name," it came a few days after the revelation of the "old name." It was "chosen friend." That really meant a lot to me, as I'll explain in a minute. But in case you are wondering whether that name is biblical or not, check out the following verses:

Greater love has no one than this, that one lay down his life for his friends. You are My friends if you do what I command you. No longer do I call you slaves, for the slave does not know what his master is doing; but I have called you friends, for all things that I have heard from My Father I have made known to you. You did not choose Me but I chose you...

John 15:13–16a

Now, I wouldn't recommend you go up to your friends and say, "You are my friends if you do what I command you." Not a great relationship strategy. But since Jesus is not only our friend but our Lord, He has every right to say that!

But the point of my sharing those verses is so you can know that I am a friend of God and so are you... if you are in Christ. And even though we came to faith in Jesus and received Him, it was actually God working in us, choosing us and drawing us to Himself. He chose us. And He chose you and me because He *wanted* us and wants to spend time with us (Mark 3:13–14). That is really cool. Because of all the times I had to take the initiative to get one of my "friends" to come over, to know that Jesus took the lead and "called me up" because He wanted to hang out with me, so to speak, means a lot. I am God's chosen friend.

So what's your "old name"? It could very well be an important part of your healing process to identify it so you can renounce it like I did. And more importantly, what's your "new name"? Of all the truths about your identity in Christ from Ephesians 1 and 1 Peter 1–2 and other places, which name is really meaningful to you on a heart level? Allowing the truth of your new identity in Christ to penetrate into the places of shame in your soul can be absolutely life-transforming.

The exercises at the end of today's devotional may be just what "the Doctor" ordered, so make sure you take unhurried time to do them.

A THOUGHT TO CHEW ON

God wants to give us a new name which expresses the truth of who we now are in Christ in a way that heals and transforms us.

A TRUTH TO REMEMBER

"As the bridegroom rejoices over the bride, so your God will rejoice over you" (Isaiah 62:5).

A QUESTION TO MULL OVER

What is your "old name"? What is your "new name"? Use the following prayer to talk to God about this matter and look forward to Him answering your prayer in the days ahead.

TALKING IT OVER WITH GOD

Dear heavenly Father, when You look at my old life without You, what do You see? What name or label or description would sum up that part of my life in Your eyes? I want to be free from having that label haunt me and rob me of joy and keep me from walking by faith according to who I am in You now.

So I ask You for discernment and understanding and thank You in advance for it. As much as I want to renounce all that I was apart from You, even more so I long to announce the truth of who I now am in You. If it would please You to reveal to my heart in a powerful and life-transforming way how You now see me, I would receive that word for freedom, healing and empowerment.

Protect me from my own speculations and imaginations as well as the enemy's counterfeit guidance. I thank You that being led by You is one of the realities of my living relationship with You. I know You love me. I love You, too. Amen.

Day 21: Unmasking the Imposter

As we wrap up these two weeks focusing on guilt and shame and God's antidote to each, I hope you are seeing the power of what He has done for you in Christ. Because of the Lord Jesus' death on the cross, His burial and resurrection, His sending of the Holy Spirit, giving of His Word and creating of the Church, the body of Christ, He has graciously given us all we need for life and godliness.

Our responsibility is to *trust* what He says and walk in the truth of what He has done for us and in us. And when it comes to the "disease" of shame, our new identity in Christ (who we really are now) is the cure. The old things are passed away, new things have come (2 Corinthians 5:17). Reading through and prayerfully thinking about who you are in Christ (see *Victory Over the Darkness* and *The Steps to Freedom in Christ* by Dr Neil T. Anderson for further help) will cause those truths to drill deep into your heart. They are true because they are straight out of God's word. And because they *are* true, you *can* believe them.

Have you ever noticed, however, that "believing the truth" can sometimes be easier said than done? In today's devotional we want to unmask one of the enemy's (Satan's) strategies designed to make trusting God harder than it is. In other words, he knows full well what God's 100 percent effective cure for shame is; he just doesn't want you to believe it.

This devil tactic can be summed up simply as "impersonating God's voice in your life." That's right. As dirty a trick as that sounds (but since when has the devil ever cared about fighting fair?), Satan and his demons will try to get you to think you are hearing from God when you are actually hearing from them. What you "hear" will likely not be audible, but will take the form of impressions, sometimes very strong impressions, ideas and thoughts.

Many of God's people sadly remain locked in a shame-based self-perception because they believe the harsh, accusing voice in their minds is actually God speaking, when it is not. So, in order to help you ferret out this lying rat of darkness, I'm going to lay out some basic principles of contrast between how God speaks to us versus how the devil does. Ready?

First, consider the "tone of voice." God's voice is the gentle, loving voice of a Father inviting, welcoming and urging our return to Him when we have sinned. The devil's voice is accusing, nagging, and mocking. It generates fear, causes confusion and projects a sense of rejection. Sometimes it even creates doubt about what is right and wrong.

Second, the work of the Holy Spirit in our minds is specific. He urges you to confess and repent of something that you have done with the assurance of forgiveness and cleansing when you do (see 1 John 1:9). The devil brings a blanketing, choking, general sense of guilt and shame as though everything is wrong and there is no clear action you can take to remedy the problem. An almost overwhelming sense of weakness and hopelessness can result.

Third, God's strategy is encouragement, letting you know you are loved by Him and urging you to believe there is hope for real life change as you rely on the Holy Spirit's power to live life well. On the other hand, the devil's tactic is discouragement. He centers his attack on you as a person, cutting your self-image to ribbons. He sends the message that you are weak, unloved, worthless, shameful, and that there is no hope of change.

Are any lights coming on so far? Maybe you are becoming aware that your concept of God as harsh, strict, rigid and unbending is simply the efforts of a cunning impersonator.

Perhaps you have listened far too long to an imposter! If so, don't get down on yourself. Just look at today as the dawning of new light in your life and the removal of one more avenue of enemy attack. And that's a very good thing!

Here's some more:

Fourth, in Christ guilt is gone and shame is removed. That is always God's message. Restoration is complete. The devil's tactic is to replay the film of past memories of sin, guilt and shame. He draws up accounts of your past sins, failures and offenses (that are already washed clean by the blood of Christ) and tries to get you to fear that they will haunt you forever, and that you will never really be free.

Fifth, God's desire is always to woo His children back to Him with kindness, tolerance and patience (see Romans 2:4). With Him there is always the promise of a new start, another chance, with new hope based on the permanent Father–child relationship He cherishes. Satan, however, disguises himself as an agent of holiness and wants you to believe that God in His holiness is so offended by your unholiness that you are unworthy of his love, unworthy to come into God's presence. In other words, the devil wants you to believe that you are a miserable sinner, rather than the glorious saint that you are.

Sixth, the Lord will guide and direct you to scriptures that encourage you, reminding you of God's unchanging promises and steadfast love. He wants us to know that He is faithful and loyal to His covenant, even when we prove faithless for a time (see 2 Timothy 2:13; 1 John 3:20). "Therefore there is now no condemnation for those who are in Christ Jesus" (Romans 8:1). On the other hand, Satan uses the Law against you, to press you to justify yourself in a vain attempt to rely on your own righteousness (remember Galatians 2:16). Therefore there is now plenty of condemnation with the devil! Sometimes he will go so far as to try and convince you that you have committed the unpardonable sin; at the very least he will try and get you to doubt that you have been 100 percent sincere in your confession so that you will end up confessing and repenting of the same things over and over again, trying "to get it right."

Seventh, God wants you to believe the facts of His word, the Bible. The devil wants you to believe that what you *feel* is true. Sometimes our feelings of doubt, fear, self-pity, God's "unfairness" and so on can "feel more true" than what the Bible says. If we believe our feelings, we play right into Satan's hand. If we know and believe the truth, we are set free (John 8:31–32)!

Finally, the Lord is always urging you to return to fellowship and communication with Himself and the body of Christ, because He knows that is where long-term joy and healing are found. The devil sows suggestions that cause you to withdraw from other Christians, thinking they are already rejecting you. In your isolation, you then feel lonely, hurt, unworthy, misunderstood, angry and rejected by others. This isolation makes you not only susceptible to a deeper spiral into sin but also makes you vulnerable to false doctrine.

Well, that ended up becoming a mini-handbook on spiritual discernment, didn't it? But I hope it's helpful to you and to those you love. I close today's and this week's topic with this powerful section of Paul's writings, which reminds us of the crucial difference between godly sorrow and repentance, which draw us back to God, and worldly sorrow (that the devil incites), that brings regret, isolation and even death:

> I now rejoice, not that you were made sorrowful,
> but that you were made sorrowful to the point of
> repentance; for you were made sorrowful according
> to the will of God, so that you might not suffer loss in
> anything through us. For the sorrow that is according

to the will of God produces a repentance without regret, leading to salvation, but the sorrow of the world produces death.

2 Corinthians 7:9–10

A THOUGHT TO CHEW ON

The devil can put impressions into our minds that masquerade as the voice of God, seeking to keep us locked in guilt and shame.

A TRUTH TO REMEMBER

"If you continue in My word, then you are truly disciples of Mine; and you will know the truth, and the truth will make you free" (John 8:31–32).

A QUESTION TO MULL OVER

As you look at your life, which strategies of the devil discussed in today's devotional has he used effectively against you? What truth about God and His word do you need to hold fast to in order to defeat the enemy's tactics?

TALKING IT OVER WITH GOD

Dear heavenly Father, most of the time I have to admit that I am clueless as to what is going on in the unseen, spiritual world around me. I live a large part of my life believing that things are pretty much up to me. When I read the Bible or go to church I'm a bit more aware of You, and I want that awareness of Your presence to grow stronger and more consistent. But today's devotional has opened my eyes to the fact that I have been largely oblivious to the reality of the unseen world of the powers of darkness. And that can't be good. How many times have

I thought that I was just battling my own thoughts when in reality I have been wrestling against dark powers... without realizing it?

Please give me discernment, Lord, so that I can choose Your truth and reject the devil's lies that are bombarding my brain. Thank You for exposing some of his tactics so that I can wage and win spiritual war and walk free from the traps of false guilt and false shame and a false view of You that the devil would want me to accept as truth. Amen.

From Fear to Faith

Day 22: God is Awake

We now come to our fourth week of *40 Days of Grace* as we look at how God's grace gives us the courage to overcome the unhealthy, controlling fears in our lives. As many have expressed in their writings over the years, courage isn't the absence of fear. Courage is doing what is right and responsible in the face of fear.

That's important to know, so you don't think we are attempting to remove all the feelings of fear from our lives, as much as we may dislike them. It isn't even wise to do so, since there are some fears that are very healthy.

Hiking in the desert mountains near Needles, California, it was a good thing – a God thing, really – to be alarmed and to come to a screeching halt when I spotted a rattlesnake sunning itself on the path about twenty feet ahead. And when I tossed a rock at it to try and get it to move and it snapped into a coiled position with its head and rattling tail up, ready to strike, my apprehension escalated into fright just as fast. I was afraid and I needed to be.

No, all fear isn't bad. Fear sends chemicals coursing through our bodies enabling us to make the "fight or flight" decision instantly and decisively, for our own protection.

But what if I went around anxiously looking out for snakes everywhere I went? Or what if I refused to go outside for fear that a rattlesnake would get me? It doesn't take a genius to see the difference. A healthy fear alerts someone to danger that is really there. That is, the threat is both *present* and *powerful* (or potent). An unhealthy fear – or what, in an acute or chronic state, is often called a "phobia" – alerts someone to danger that is imaginary, solely in the mind of the one with the fear. In other words, the fear object – in the mind of the fearful person – is both *present* and *powerful*, when in reality at least one of those two attributes does not actually exist.

Let's go back to snakes. Well, let's not, literally – but you know what I mean. First, are all snakes dangerous? No, many aren't. In fact, I've never seen a poisonous snake around my house in twelve years, though I've seen plenty of snakes. So the truth is that probably the majority of snakes are not "powerful" or "potent." Second, are there snakes crawling over every square inch of ground… kind of like that horrible snake pit in which Indiana Jones found himself in *Raiders of the Lost Ark*? No, of course not. So snakes aren't particularly "present" either, at least not the reptile kind. (Sorry, couldn't resist.)

Therefore, snakes are not everywhere present and most are not powerful at all. That's why a person with a healthy fear of snakes is not afraid to walk around outside, nor does he or she live in the constant fear of being bitten. But to someone with an irrational fear that has developed inside their minds, where an unreal picture of life can breed, the world becomes a place teeming with the nasty, slithering varmints lurking in the shadows, just waiting to jump out and bite. That kind of belief would scare anyone!

Now, obviously this week's devotionals are not principally about overcoming the fear of snakes. Nor are they just about conquering phobias, though that is hopefully part of the package. The reality is that just about all of us struggle with some kind of unhealthy fear at some level. Don't think so? Well, then, just get out of your chair and walk down the street and share the gospel with all your neighbors.

You didn't do it, did you? See what I mean?

The point is that none of us walks by faith 100 percent of the time. All of us, to some degree, allow fears to control us and keep us from doing what is right and responsible. In other words, you need God's grace to live courageously, even if you might not be aware of anything that might be called a phobia in your life.

An important factor to consider with irrational fears is that they seem very real to those experiencing them. Therefore, it is futile to try to cure someone of *irrational fears* with *rational arguments*, like "There's nothing to be afraid of" or "It's all in your mind" or "See? Nobody else is afraid, so neither should you be." You get the picture. In response to the last of those feeble attempts at persuasion I just listed, the fearful one would likely be thinking, "Well, it's obvious everyone else is clueless!"

I've done a lot of thinking on the subject of fear over the years, and there are a few "bottom line" conclusions I have come to that I think will be helpful to look at as we start this week.

The first conclusion is that fear and faith are like the two opposite ends of a seesaw or teeter totter. When one end goes up, the other goes down... and vice versa. In the same way, when fear goes up, faith goes down and vice versa. Fear robs us of faith and faith robs fear of its power to control us.

The second conclusion is that the ultimate solution to any unhealthy fear is to have a true view of God and His ultimate *power* and constant, caring *presence* in all situations. You see, fearful people feel very alone, abandoned, isolated, "on their own," vulnerable and helpless. They don't remember that God is nearby and very willing and able to help.

We haven't done an equation in a while, so I'll let my "left-brained self" loose for a moment, once again:

- Threatening (or perceived threatening) situation + feeling alone and helpless = Fear
- Same situation + knowing God cares and is present and powerful = Faith

You kind of get that sense from my favorite quote on courage. It comes from the pen of the author Victor Hugo. He wrote:

> Have courage for the great sorrows of life and patience for the small ones, and when you have laboriously accomplished your daily tasks, go to sleep in peace. God is awake.

It helps me to walk by faith and not in fear by remembering that God is awake and never sleeps and never leaves my side.

I remember one night when my young son, Brian, was feverishly sick and agitated, scared, tossing and turning all night long. I sat by the side of his bed watching to make sure he was not in danger, occasionally placing my hand on his forehead to see if his fever was worsening, praying for his healing. I was determined to be there for him and to be able to lovingly, reassuringly meet his gaze should he open his eyes to see if I was still there. Numerous times he did open his eyes, and once he knew I hadn't left, he closed them again and went back to sleep. All was well. No need to fear. Dad was awake and there.

We'll wrap up today's devotional with a couple of Bible verses well worth memorizing. The first one is the assurance of someone looking to God for help. The second is God speaking directly to you and me about our fears:

> When I remember You on my bed,
> I meditate on You in the night watches,
> For You have been my help,

And in the shadow of Your wings I sing for joy.
My soul clings to You;
Your right hand upholds me.

Psalm 63:6–8

Do not fear, for I am with you;
Do not anxiously look about you, for I am your God.
I will strengthen you, surely I will help you,
Surely I will uphold you with My righteous right hand.

Isaiah 41:10

When we are afraid, we run to God and we cling to Him desperately, afraid to let go lest He leave us all alone. Child of God, it is not you clinging to Him that saves you; what saves you is that He is holding you up with His right hand. You can sleep in peace. No need to fear. God is awake.

A THOUGHT TO CHEW ON

When faith goes up, fear goes down. And vice versa.

A TRUTH TO REMEMBER

"Do not fear, for I am with you" (Isaiah 41:10).

A QUESTION TO MULL OVER

Ask God to show you any people that you shy away from out of fear or situations that you avoid out of dread or apprehension. Do you have any fears that have been there for a long time, where you would really like God's grace to make you courageous?

TALKING IT OVER WITH GOD

Dear heavenly Father, when I am in touch with truth and seeing things as they really are, I have to admit that life on my own and in my own strength is a pretty scary proposition. There are so many variables and things out of my control. Many times, though, I have to admit I can still be lulled into a state of smug complacency until something in life or on the news rocks my world and shocks me back into the reality that nothing aside from You is a sure thing. And yet I don't want to live life controlled by fear either. I want to live with the constant awareness that You are there and You care and that You uphold me with Your righteous right hand.

Please make me aware of the things that rob me of faith and keep me in the grip of anxiety or fear. I look forward to living even more in the way that is right and responsible, filled with the courage to face my fears by Your grace. Thank You that You are awake. Amen.

Day 23: The Weapon of Worship

I was scared. As I stared up at the thirty-foot-high cliff that we were all supposed to climb, I began to sweat. Others who were experienced at rock climbing and belaying explained to me how safe it was. Yeah, right. The guy who was climbing the cliff before it was my turn, fell about ten feet flat on his back because his belayer was a little bit be-lazy. That didn't exactly bolster my confidence! Fortunately, neither the climber nor the belayer (on whom the climber landed!) was hurt.

Well, like a nightmare come true, it was finally my turn to go up. All kinds of fears ricocheted around in my brain:

Will I have that same belayer?

What if I can't find a foothold or handhold?

Am I going to look like a complete dork up there?

Am I strong enough to do this?

Will I panic?

What if I fall?

Will anybody come to my funeral?

You know, important stuff like that.

Well, not so bravely I started up the cliff. At first it wasn't too tough. There were plenty of places to grab onto with my feet and hands. I was halfway up the cliff before I knew it.

"Hey, this isn't bad at all," I said to myself.

Famous last words. Suddenly I looked up and saw nowhere to go. I was stuck.

People started yelling encouraging things from below, like: "Don't panic! You're all right!"

Then why didn't I feel all right? My legs and arms were starting to shake with fatigue. It was all I could do to keep from yelling back, "That's easy for you to say! You're not clinging to the side of a cliff fifteen to twenty feet above the ground, you bozo!" But I didn't say that. After all, I'm a Christian.

"Whatever you do, don't look down!" That was another helpful hint.

Why not? I wondered. Is Igor the Sleeping Belayer down there?

"Reach up with your right hand! There's a place about two feet above and to the right of your head! You can't see it, but it's there!"

Recognizing the voice of my boss, I wracked my brain: Have I given him any reason to hate me lately?

Realizing that my strength was draining away fast as I was clutching the face of the cliff for dear life, I decided to go for it.

I missed.

Exhausted and discouraged, I began to have this really eerie sensation. I'm going to fall. This is it. I'm never going to see my wife again!

In despair I cried out, "I'm falling!" What else would you say?

And then it was over. There I was, dangling in midair off the face of the cliff… completely safe. The ropes had held me up!

I actually began to enjoy it up there. What a relief! I didn't have to toil and sweat trying to climb up that stupid cliff. I could just hang around and relax. That lasted about fifteen seconds until my boss told me to get back on the wall and finish the climb.

Oh yeah, minor details. But I finally made it. After one more fall and about five or ten more minutes of exhausting climbing, I dragged myself up over the crest of the cliff and sprawled out on the flat area at the top in glorious victory!

Prior to the climb I had known in my head that my boss knew what he was doing in the area of rock climbing. I knew that the ropes were strong enough to hold me. But all that head knowledge only turned to heart knowledge when I fell and the ropes came through for me. After that I could face the climb without fear.

I'm glad that we spent the past two weeks in this devotional seeking to help you get past guilt and shame. Those things drive us away from God in fear of His anger, rejection or punishment. And if we are afraid of God somehow hurting us or we are mistrustful of His caring, loving presence, where will we go when we are afraid?

The apostle John's words really help us know we need not be afraid of God:

> We have come to know and have believed the love
> which God has for us. God is love, and the one who
> abides in love abides in God, and God abides in him…
> There is no fear in love; but perfect love casts out fear,
> because fear involves punishment, and the one who
> fears is not perfected in love.
>
> 1 John 4:16, 18

When we are afraid, we need to know that we can trust God. Why can we trust God? Because He loves us. We are His children and the punishment we deserved fell on Christ and will never fall on us. John also wrote:

> See how great a love the Father has bestowed on us, that
> we would be called children of God; and such we are.
>
> 1 John 3:1

We are indeed children of God, safe and secure, no matter how tough the climbs that face us in life might be. God knows the way. He *is* the way. He is your strength for the climb. And if you happen to fall, the steadfast ropes of His love and faithfulness will hold you up. King David wrote:

> The steps of a man are established by the LORD,
> And He delights in his way.
> When he falls, he will not be hurled headlong,
> Because the LORD is the One who holds his hand.
>
> Psalm 37:23–24

Now, this is where it gets really cool, because the Lord in His grace has given us a VERY powerful weapon in our fight against fear. Remember: it is knowing and believing that our all-mighty, ever-caring, completely-loving and always-present God is with us that gives us courage. And the best way to acknowledge His presence is worship! Worship is our weapon.

When you seek God in worship and proclaim His faithfulness, love and power, fear flees! Listen in as King David shares what he learned in life. It should really encourage you:

> I will bless the LORD at all times;
> His praise shall continually be in my mouth.
> My soul will make its boast in the LORD;
> The humble will hear it and rejoice.
> O magnify the LORD with me,
> And let us exalt His name together.
> I sought the LORD, and He answered me,
> And delivered me from all my fears.
> They looked to Him and were radiant,
> and their faces will never be ashamed.
>
> Psalm 34:1–5

Worship is a weapon of war and the battle against fear is just that – a war. But as we seek the Lord and worship Him continually, He will rescue us from *all* our fears. And your glowing face will tell the story.

A THOUGHT TO CHEW ON

Worship is a powerful weapon of war against fear.

A TRUTH TO REMEMBER

"There is no fear in love; but perfect love casts out fear" (1 John 4:18a).

A QUESTION TO MULL OVER

How can you incorporate worship of God more into your day? It is often when our minds are idle that fears come. Ask God to show you creative ways to worship rather than worry!

TALKING IT OVER WITH GOD

Dear heavenly Father, I know that if I could actually see You and Your greatness, all my fears would melt away. Since seeing You physically isn't possible, please open my eyes of faith to be aware of Your very real presence as I worship. Thank You that I can always trust in You and that there is no need to fear Your punishment because You love me. I am Your child. I will seek You and trust You to deliver me from all my fears. Amen.

Day 24: So, What is the Fear of God?

I admit that it's sometimes really hard to fully wrap our minds around this Christian life. In some ways that is to be expected, since God is so much higher than we are. So it shouldn't surprise us, I guess, if at times we're left scratching our heads.

In case you hadn't noticed, God's kingdom is pretty much counter-intuitive. The way to be exalted is to humble yourself. The way to true strength is through weakness. The way to save your life is to lose it. And so on. There is and always will be an element of paradox, even mystery, when it comes to God and how we relate to Him.

This is one of those places.

We just got through telling you yesterday that, as John wrote, "there is no fear in love," referring to our relationship with the God who loves us. And then today it might seem like we are totally contradicting ourselves by talking about "the fear of God" as a healthy, necessary thing!

Trust me. I'm really not trying to confuse you. Maybe this would be a good place to pray:

> *Dear Father, I thank You for Your love and that I am Your child by Your amazing grace. You really are saddened when Your kids are so guilt-ridden or ashamed or fearful of You that they run and hide rather than seek You. In fact, You are so warm-hearted and tender-hearted that You are absolutely filled with delight when I come to You. It disturbs me a bit, then, when I hear that "The fear of the LORD is the beginning of wisdom" (Proverbs 9:10). Would you please give me understanding of what it means to fear You and how that fear is actually the fear that dispels all other fears? Thank You. Amen.*

Let's start out with stating what is obvious… at least obvious to anybody who takes the Bible seriously. "The fear of the Lord" is a theme throughout both the Old and New Testaments. Proverbs 9:10, that I referred to in the prayer above, is just one of numerous places in the Old Testament that talk about this subject. But what about the New Testament? Here's an example:

> So then, my beloved, just as you have always obeyed, not as in my presence only, but now much more in my absence, work out your salvation with fear and trembling; for it is God who is at work in you, both to will and to work for His good pleasure
>
> Philippians 2:12–13

The reality that the God of the universe is active and personally invested in molding our hearts and moving in our lives ought to give us pause to consider our responsibility to cooperate with and not resist Him. It is not a trivial thing to stand in His way.

And, just in case you think that scripture is an isolated incident or "taken out of context," 1 Peter 1:17 reinforces the concept of the fear of the Lord:

> If you address as Father the One who impartially judges according to each one's work, conduct yourselves in fear during the time of your stay on earth.

The apostle makes it clear that there ought to be an element of fear and trepidation in our lives as we look forward to the throne of God where our works will be judged impartially by God. That is actually a very healthy fear. Peter goes on to reinforce his argument in the verses that follow by reminding the reader that God has made an almost unbelievable investment in us... buying us out of slavery to our old way of living through the shed blood of Christ. And that blood is far more precious than all the silver and gold in the world! God clearly expects us to live out, by His strength, this high calling we have.

Now notice something. God is not going to judge us for our sins. He already did that in Christ on the cross. He will never bring up those things again with us. What He will do is evaluate the quality of our deeds (1 Corinthians 3:10–15 teaches that), and that coming judgment is meant to motivate us to do what pleases Him in His strength and for His glory.

OK, hopefully you get the message. Fearing God is something we should do. So what exactly *is* the fear of God? And how does fearing God help us overcome all other fears? Maybe some personal recollections will help at this point.

My parents, thank God, were never abusive of me. But they did lovingly and firmly discipline me. They let me know who was in charge when I got out of line. If I mouthed off to my mom or disobeyed my dad, I knew something not so fun was going to happen. Maybe I would be sent to my room or spanked or (the worst of all!) forbidden to eat dessert or watch TV.

I also believed, as a kid, that my dad would protect me and beat up anybody that might try to hurt me. If I were scared of burglars, I drew great comfort from watching my dad's towering form lock all the doors and confidently turn out the lights. He was strong. His voice was powerful. He was invincible, in my thinking.

Because of these things I had a great respect for, admiration of and healthy fear of my parents... especially my dad. But I wasn't afraid of him. I knew he loved me because he'd play baseball with me and buy me stuff and pick me up and rub his whiskery face against my smooth cheeks (a bit irritating but still cool!). And he always smelled like Old Spice cologne. That, to me, was the smell of a man you could count on. I could've and would've done a commercial for that company!

I remember one night we were having a huge thunderstorm. Lightning hit our house and set on fire the nightlight right by my bed. I was terrified and screamed, "Fire! Fire!" It took all of a glass of water to put out the fire, but there was no way I was going to stay in my bed alone that night! So I jumped in bed between my mom and dad and knew I was safe. After all, I was next to my dad, and he was invincible!

Are you getting the picture? Can you see how just understanding the love of God, without seeing how infinitely powerful, majestic and strong He is, would not fully help you overcome fear?

Our God can do anything. Nothing is too difficult for Him (Jeremiah 32:17). Read these words and stand in awe of His power and receive the reassurance that (unlike my dad) He truly *is* invincible – a reality that makes you tremble at His greatness while assuring you that you are safe in His arms:

> "I love You, O LORD, my strength."
> The LORD is my rock and my fortress and my deliverer,
> My God, my rock, in whom I take refuge;
> My shield and the horn of my salvation, my stronghold.
> I call upon the LORD, who is worthy to be praised,
> And I am saved from my enemies.
>
> Psalm 18:1–3

To fear God is to stand in awe of Him. To tremble at His power and greatness and yet run to Him when you are afraid, finding Him to be a sanctuary… a place of safety and protection (see Isaiah 8:11–14). No question about it. God, who spoke the entire universe into existence and will one day destroy it and create a new heavens and earth (2 Peter 3:10–13), is worthy of our deepest reverence and awe and fear… because He purchased us and is working in us for His good pleasure and purposes. That realization should make us live our lives in obedience, spotless and blameless (2 Peter 3:14). The fear of the Lord is to hate evil and turn away from it (Proverbs 8:13; 16:6), because God hates it and will one day wipe it all out.

But that deep, deep respect for His power and holiness also wraps itself around us like a warm comforter on a cold night, knowing that no enemy of ours, visible or invisible, is any match for Him. I close with the "preamble" to the powerful Psalm 91. You ought to read it all, but here are the first four verses. The psalm is like an antibiotic against the "bacteria" of unhealthy fear:

> He who dwells in the shelter of the Most High
> Will abide in the shadow of the Almighty.
> I will say to the LORD, "My refuge and my fortress,
> My God in whom I trust!"
> For it is He who delivers you from the snare of the
> trapper And from the deadly pestilence.
> He will cover you with His pinions,
> And under His wings you may seek refuge;
> His faithfulness is a shield and bulwark.

A THOUGHT TO CHEW ON

The healthy fear of God wipes out all other unhealthy fears.

A TRUTH TO REMEMBER

"I call upon the LORD, who is worthy to be praised, and I am saved from my enemies" (Psalm 18:3).

A QUESTION TO MULL OVER

Think about how powerful God is. Come up with a list of things that God and nobody else can do. How does that knowledge not only make you tremble at His power but also give you great assurance that He, in His love, will protect you from all other fears?

TALKING IT OVER WITH GOD

Dear All-Powerful Father, what an incredible thing to know that You really are a Dad who can do anything and whip anybody and that there is nothing in this world that I can see or can't see that is any match for You. I come running to You… trembling at Your awesome majesty and holiness, but laughing with joy also because I know Your loving arms are wide open to me. I renounce all fears except the healthy fear of You. Jesus, You are Victor and in You I am, too! Amen.

Day 25: A Death Blow to Death

When it comes right down to it, our fears basically boil down to a couple of things: our severe aversion to pain and suffering, and our terror of the unknown, of things out of our control and beyond our understanding. That may be why the number one fear that people have, at least in America, is the fear of public speaking. Talk about the possibility of suffering painful embarrassment or shame and of things (like an audience!) being out of our control – that's it!

Basically, we humans like to feel safe, comfortable, and "in control." And so if we perceive anything as threatening our safety, comfort and ability to control, we experience some level of fear… anything from a vague uneasiness (on the low side) to abject terror and panic (on the high side).

Remember how we discussed earlier this week that when we are afraid, we are viewing something or someone as being both *present* and *powerful*? That is, the thing we are afraid of is perceived to be nearby (or approaching), with the capacity to harm us. In other words, we feel vulnerable.

Here's a very interesting question. What do you think happens to fear if just one of those two attributes of the fear object – either its *presence* or its *power* (or potency) – is removed? We'll try and answer that question over the next couple of days.

Take the fear of death as an example. Is death a legitimate fear object? That is, should we fear death? Now, to be perfectly honest, if someone does not have the Son of God and the eternal life He brings (see 1 John 5:11–13), then the fear of death would be a *very* legitimate fear!

But is the "fear of death" a legitimate fear for a true follower of Christ? Notice I didn't ask, "Is the fear of death a *real* fear for a true follower of Christ?" There is no doubt that many believers in Jesus are really afraid of death. You could say that they are scared to death of death. The question is, stated another way, "Is there any reason why a Christian *should be* afraid to die?"

The answer, which you probably intuitively know, is *no*. Why not? Isn't death a very real presence? Isn't death really powerful? I mean, speaking of things that are potent and can harm us, it's kind of hard to harm somebody more than killing them, isn't it?

Let's look closely at these two attributes of death... its *presence* and its *power*. First, its presence. No matter how healthy you may think you are, death can come at almost any time. A traffic accident. A heart attack. A stroke. Something else.

When I hit fifty years old, being a golfer of sorts, I found it helpful to figure out where on the "golf course of life" I was located, statistically speaking. Turns out I was on the twelfth or thirteenth hole. But as I reflected on that statistical reality, it occurred to me that I might be on the eighteenth green and not know it. That's really true for all of us. Unless Jesus comes back first, we're all going to die and none of us knows precisely when that will be. Hebrews 9:27 says:

> And inasmuch as it is appointed for men to die once and after this comes judgment...

There you have it. The reality of death is always present for us. Despite all the vitamins we take, the exercises we do, the cosmetic surgery we undergo to try and fake ourselves and others into thinking we're younger than we are, we are all going to die sooner or later. Exciting news, right? I'm sure you'd be really eager to invite me to one of your parties.

The point is that if we are trying to remove one of those two attributes of death – either its *presence* or its *power* – trying to remove its presence is a dead-end street (pun intended).

But what about its *power*? Ah, this is where grace comes in. Feast your eyes on the following scriptures and see what conclusions you can draw in regard to the power of death over a true follower of Christ:

> "Death is swallowed up in victory. O death, where is your victory? O death, where is your sting?" The sting of death is sin, and the power of sin is the law; but thanks be to God, who gives us the victory through our Lord Jesus Christ.
>
> 1 Corinthians 15:54b–57

> Jesus said to her, "I am the resurrection and the life; he who believes in Me will live even if he dies, and everyone who lives and believes in Me will never die. Do you believe this?"
>
> John 11:25–26

> Therefore, since the children share in flesh and blood, He Himself [Jesus] likewise also partook of the same, that through death He might render powerless him who had the power of death, that is, the devil, and might free those who through fear of death were subject to slavery all their lives.
>
> Hebrews 2:14–15

So, according to the Bible, what has happened to death's *power* over Christ's followers? That's right; it no longer exists – that is, in the sense of its capacity to harm. Its victory has been snatched away. It doesn't win. It doesn't have the last word. Life does. Jesus, who is the resurrection and the life, has the final say, not the devil, and physical death simply becomes a gateway for the follower of Christ into an eternity of eternal life, in a place far better than this.

The apostle Paul wrote:

> For to me, to live is Christ and to die is gain. But if
> I am to live on in the flesh [here on earth], this will
> mean fruitful labor for me; and I do not know which
> to choose. But I am hard-pressed from both directions,
> having the desire to depart and be with Christ, for that
> is very much better...

Philippians 1:21–23

Did you catch those words: "to die is *gain*" and "having the desire to depart and be with Christ, for *that is very much better*"?

For the true believer in Jesus, there is nothing to fear from death. It is going to be awesome on the other side. And even though we don't fully know what heaven will be like, it is going to be a whole lot better than this place, I can tell you that much!

Still, you might complain that though the destination of death is going to be tremendous, the journey to get there could be most unpleasant. True enough. But should we allow ourselves to be controlled by the "fear of dying"? Is that something we should worry about, letting it steal our joy? Certainly not. In fact, Philippians 4:6 basically tells us not to worry about anything, but rather to be thankful and pray about everything. If we do, God's peace and not our anxiety will reign.

One principle that really helps in dealing with fears is that fretting about what might happen ahead of time is absolutely useless. There is no grace given by God in response to our worries about the future. But He does promise us grace for the tough times we experience in the present. Paul found this out and shared what he'd learned with us so we can experience faith in God's promised grace rather than fear about life's possible pain:

Because of the surpassing greatness of the revelations,
for this reason, to keep me from exalting myself, there
was given to me a thorn in the flesh, a messenger of
Satan to torment me – to keep me from exalting myself!
Concerning this I implored the Lord three times that it
might leave me. And He has said to me, "My grace is
sufficient for you, for power is perfected in weakness."
Most gladly, therefore, I will rather boast about my
weaknesses, so that the power of Christ may dwell in
me… for when I am weak, then I am strong.

2 Corinthians 12:7–10

In Christ there need be no fear of death, for Jesus is the
resurrection and the life… and we are in Him and He is in us!
And there need be no fear of dying either, because what lies
on the other side is glorious and the path to get there will be
most assuredly paved with grace.

A THOUGHT TO CHEW ON

God's grace is sufficient to carry us through anything life
throws at us.

A TRUTH TO REMEMBER

"For to me, to live is Christ and to die is gain" (Philippians 1:21).

A QUESTION TO MULL OVER

The fear of death can be sort of an umbrella under which a
whole bunch of other fears hide… like the fear of heights; fear
of enclosed spaces; fear of the dark; fear of various animals;
fear of getting sick; fear of being victimized by crime, and so
on. How does knowing that Christ is the resurrection and the
life and that His grace is sufficient for you grant you grace to
overcome your fear?

TALKING IT OVER WITH GOD

Dear Father, You know if there are fears that lurk in the shadowy places of my soul. And You know why they're there. Would You please open my eyes to these things that I might renounce these fears so I can watch my faith in You grow? I thank You that Your peace, that goes far beyond what I can understand, will guard my heart and mind from the attacks of fear and anxiety that can seem so overwhelming. Your peace is stronger than anxiety. Faith in You is bigger than any fear.

I choose today to no longer believe that what I feel and fear is supreme. Christ is supreme. I dethrone all my fears and place the Lord Jesus Christ where He belongs in my life... on the throne. And thank You, Lord, that it is a wonderful throne of grace that I can approach any time of the day or night when I need your help, and You will welcome me there. Amen.

Day 26: Breaking Fear's Teeth

I had just finished teaching a weekend conference on freedom at a church in Illinois, and I was enjoying the afterglow of worship, discussion and stories of how lives had been touched and changed during those two days. It never ceases to amaze me how even in an event that only extends over about twenty-four hours, the Lord Jesus brings breakthroughs that change the course of lives. I guess I shouldn't be surprised, though. He Himself said, "So if the Son makes you free, you will be free indeed" (John 8:36).

Not everyone's liberation from bondage is so swift, I realize. And even those who experience the power of Christ to set free during such a weekend have likely been on God's operating table for quite a while already. We just never know when the breakthrough will come, and sometimes we are privileged to be there when it happens.

After this particular conference, the topic of discussion turned toward overcoming fear. It turns out, the last time we checked, that anxiety disorders were the number one mental health problem in America. And it wouldn't surprise me if they are at the top of the list for other Western nations as well. From the liveliness of our discussion that day, it was obvious fear was a big issue for the believers in this group.

At one point, a woman who appeared to be in her forties spoke up.

"I have been very afraid of the dark for as far back as I can remember," she began. "But I have never understood why until this weekend.

"Whenever I drive home at night, I get out of my car and run as fast as I can to the front door. I'm scared to death until I can get inside or turn on a light."

Actually it's very reasonable for someone to feel a bit

uneasy when alone in a dark place at night. This would obviously be especially true for a woman. But this lady's emotional response was clearly extreme... far beyond a healthy guardedness.

"The Lord brought to mind a memory that I hadn't thought about for a long time. When I was four years old, my friends and I went trick or treating on Halloween night. As we walked from door to door, there was a man following us in the shadows. We got really scared... so much so that eventually we told somebody and they called the police.

"Now that I think back about it, ever since that time I have been terrified of the dark."

Once this woman identified the source of her fear, she renounced the fear, declaring that God had not given her a spirit of fear, but of power, love and a sound mind (see 2 Timothy 1:7). She could tell that the back of her fear was broken; its teeth had been shattered, and she was overjoyed. We all prayed for her that Christ would become even more real to her as her Protector and that her faith in God would grow in those places where growth had been stunted by fear's control.

What about you?

Are you afraid of things that others don't particularly struggle with? Do you sometimes wonder why fear has been a major player in your life for so long? Is it possible that your fear can be traced back to something that happened when you were young?

As crazy as it might sound, a negative, controlling fear can seem like a "safe place" for us. We trust this unhealthy fear to protect us, keeping us away from situations where we are convinced we'll be harmed. The problem is that this is actually a very bad deal. Unhealthy fears actually box us in and steal the joy of life while promising protection. And sometimes we are sadly willing to accept the suffocation of our lives to gain what feels like, but isn't, security.

When something has a grip on us and negatively influences our personality over an extended period of time, we call that a "stronghold." Unhealthy fear that controls us and that we have come to trust in, is a stronghold. Here's an easy way to remember what a "stronghold" is. A stronghold is something that has a *strong hold* on you. It's not rocket science.

Strongholds can form slowly over time due to the type of environment we grow up in or they can develop rapidly due to serious trauma. The beginning of this lady's fear of the dark started with a traumatic event, and was likely reinforced during her life as her mind became increasingly programmed to think fearfully. It took knowing the truth that Jesus was bigger than her fear to break its strong hold over her.

Fear is like a constricting snake. A python, for instance, first bites its victim, enabling it to hold on, and then it wraps its coils around its prey, gradually suffocating it. Fear can do the same thing with us, depending upon how much we succumb to its pressure. Somehow it gets a hold on us (as in the case of the scary stalker of that four-year-old girl on Halloween night), and then it gradually tightens its grip... seeking to spread its faith-robbing influence into more and more areas of our lives. We can become fearful of abandonment, rejection, failure, trying new things, confrontation, people (we'll talk about that for the next two days), Satan, life, death, and everything in between.

If fear has a strong hold on you, you might want to consider picking up the book, *Freedom from Fear*, that Dr Neil Anderson and I wrote. It handles this subject extensively.

For now, why not ask God how the "snake" of fear first "bit" you? Get someplace quiet where you can write down the things that come to your mind as you pray.

For example, are you afraid of Satan? Many Christians are. Ask the Lord to show you if there was a movie or some music or an image or a book or occult game or practice or some incident you encountered that spawned that fear. Sometimes a dark, foreboding presence can come into our room at night and scare the living daylights out of us when we are children.

It's important to note, that though our adversary, the devil, prowls around like a roaring lion (1 Peter 5:8), nowhere in the Bible does it tell us to be afraid of Satan. In fact, as you "submit therefore to God" and "resist the devil", he *will* flee from you (see James 4:7). Why? Because Jesus defeated Satan at the cross, and Christ is in you and you are in Him! Jesus came to destroy the devil's works (1 John 3:8), including those in your life. The devil knows he has been beaten by Jesus but he waits until we exercise and stand in our authority in Christ before he gives up.

Discovering the root cause of your fear of the devil (or anything else, for that matter) will enable you to break fear's teeth and release its grip on your life. And God is most able and certainly very willing to show you any root cause. Believe me, it is sure a lot easier to grow up spiritually without some stupid snake wrapped around your life!

You want to know something really powerful? Jesus said that knowing the truth would set you free (John 8:32). You might remember that from an earlier devotional. If knowing truth sets you free (and Jesus said it does), then what keeps us trapped, in bondage to fear? Believing lies! Listen to the wisdom in these words from the apostle Paul:

> Therefore I urge you, brethren, by the mercies of God, to present your bodies a living and holy sacrifice, acceptable to God, which is your spiritual service of worship. And do not be conformed to this world, but be

> transformed by the renewing of your mind, so that you
> may prove what the will of God is, that which is good
> and acceptable and perfect.
>
> Romans 12:1–2

We are conformed to this world when we believe its lies. The key to a transformed life is a mind made new by the truth. So here's the punch line in breaking the teeth of fear: Every unhealthy, controlling fear in our life is there because we are believing one or more lies. Identify the lie(s), choose the truth instead, and the teeth of that fear are shattered!

Realizing that lies that we have believed for a long time can "feel like" or "seem like" the truth, we heartily recommend that you find a brother or sister in Christ who is mature and knows God's word well, who will sit with you while you go through the following process. He or she can pray for you, help you stay on track and identify the lies that you might not recognize as lies.

Here's the simple process:

- Ask God to show you the unhealthy fears that have been controlling you. Write them down as they come to mind. Renounce those fears, one by one, knowing that God has not given you a spirit of fear, but of power, love and a sound mind (see 2 Timothy 1:7).

- Ask the Lord to show you the reason(s) the fear is there. Be prepared to confess any sinful or unwise behavior on your part, thanking Him for His forgiveness (1 John 1:9).

- Ask the Lord to show you any lies that you have believed that were the result of your fear or that help to "fuel" that fear even now. Renounce those lies one by one.

- Ask the Lord to show you biblical truth that you can continue to think about (and thus renew your mind) so that your life can be transformed by faith and not be suffocated by fear.

Need some final encouragement to overcome your fears? Do you wonder if you're strong enough? Here's another shot in the arm of "spiritual adrenaline" from our friend, Paul:

> But in all these things we overwhelmingly conquer through Him who loved us. For I am convinced that neither death, nor life, nor angels, nor principalities [demons], nor things present, nor things to come, nor powers, nor height, nor depth, nor any other created thing, will be able to separate us from the love of God, which is in Christ Jesus our Lord.
>
> Romans 8:37–39

A THOUGHT TO CHEW ON

Knowing truth sets us free. Believing lies keeps us in bondage.

A TRUTH TO REMEMBER

"For God has not given us a spirit of timidity, but of power and love and discipline" (2 Timothy 1:7).

A QUESTION TO MULL OVER

What are the lies that you are believing that feed your fear and fuel its power over you? What truth of God will set you free?

TALKING IT OVER WITH GOD

Dear faithful Father, grant me the grace to face my fears; the discernment to discover the lies behind them; the humility to confess any wrong behavior on my part that has resulted in or from my fears; the faith to renounce these fears; the wisdom to know the truth that sets me free; and the courage to walk in that truth from this time forward. Amen.

Day 27: The Invisible Line

It's normal for husbands to want to please their wives. That's a noble thing, but sometimes quite challenging. I ran into something pretty funny. It's the questions most feared by men if asked by their wives. Three of them are:

- Do I look fat?
- Do you think she's prettier than me?
- What would you do if I died?

Each question represents a relational minefield if answered incorrectly.

For example, it is recommended that men not answer the dreaded "Do I look fat?" question these ways:

- Compared to what?
- A little extra weight looks good on you.
- I've seen fatter.

How about question number two? Here are some responses to avoid:

- Yes, but you have a better personality.
- Not as pretty as you were at her age.
- Define "pretty."

The third question is an absolute no-win for the guy. Here's a possible dialogue stemming from that one:

WOMAN: What would you do if I died?

MAN: I don't know.

WOMAN: Would you get married again?

MAN: Definitely not.

WOMAN: Why not? Don't you like being married?

MAN *(beginning to sweat)*: Of course I like being married.
WOMAN: Then why wouldn't you marry again?
MAN *(relieved a bit)*: OK, I'll get married.
WOMAN *(with a hurt expression on her face)*: You would?
MAN *(feeling cornered)*: Um, could we maybe change the subject?[7]

The old adage says that "You can't please all the people all the time." True words. In fact, if you try to do that you'll go crazy.

Funny thing, though. There are quite a few Christians who live as if they believe a truly mature believer in Christ is "someone who knows the Bible really well and is nice to everybody."

Where did that idea come from? If you read any of the four gospels you will certainly not get the impression that Jesus was "nice" to everybody... if by "nice" you mean saying what people want to hear and making everyone happy. More often than not you get the idea that Jesus only cared about saying what people *needed* to hear and in the process often made them very unhappy.

Remember this story?

As He was setting out on a journey, a man ran up to Him and knelt before Him, and asked Him, "Good Teacher, what shall I do to inherit eternal life?" And Jesus said to him, "Why do you call Me good? No one is good except God alone. You know the commandments, 'Do not murder, Do not commit adultery, Do not steal, Do not bear false witness, Do not defraud, Honor your father and mother.'" And he said to Him, "Teacher, I have kept all these things from my youth up." Looking at him, Jesus felt a love for him and said to him, "One thing you lack: go and sell all you possess and give to the poor, and you will have treasure in heaven; and

come, follow Me." But at these words he was saddened,
and he went away grieving, for he was one who owned
much property.

Mark 10:17-22

Jesus was clearly not in the business of pleasing people. He
had no fear of man nor was His ultimate goal to get people to
like Him. For many of us, were we in Jesus' sandals, we would
have felt guilty for causing the man sadness and grief. Having
second thoughts about what we said, we would have run after
the man, apologizing for how we made him feel, rephrasing
our words in order to soften the blow. Jesus never did that. He
knew that He was only responsible to speak the truth in love;
He never took personal responsibility for people's reactions to
what He said. People pleasers often feel very responsible for
the emotions of others. They are driven and feel compelled to
make sure others are happy.

The lie that people pleasers have come to believe (though
they may not realize it) is that their happiness is dependent
upon the approval of other people. Can you see how that is
not freedom at all, but is in fact bondage?

When you fear man, you aren't free to fully express your
opinions or feelings. You are more concerned about how
people will react. People pleasers tend to be good people
readers. They have learned how to intuitively gauge the risk/
reward likelihood of opening their mouths. "Will they think
less of me? Reject me? Be disappointed in me? Not trust me as
much? Will I lose my job? Will I lose a friend?" Very often they
end up remaining quiet.

I really believe there is some kind of invisible line that
God wants us all to cross over where we come to fear God
more than people. In that place we are willing and able to
be honest, real people as opposed to being conformed to the

image that we imagine will make us feel comfortable and safe from controversy and acceptable to our friends.

Being *courageous* is the theme of this week. You will find no more courageous Man in all of history than Jesus. He was totally secure – in who He was, in what His mission was, in the guaranteed success of His mission and in His ultimate destination – so that He did not fear man in the least. Proverbs 29:25 says:

> The fear of man brings a snare,
> But he who trusts in the LORD will be exalted.

The apostle Paul at some point in his life and ministry crossed that invisible line into fearless faith, even confronting the apostle Peter in public about Peter's hypocrisy. Paul wrote:

> For am I now seeking the favor of men, or of God? Or
> am I striving to please men? If I were still trying to
> please men, I would not be a bond-servant of Christ.
>
> Galatians 1:10

The grace of God empowers us to become more and more like Jesus, and that includes being courageous like Him, unencumbered by the fear of man. Tomorrow we will look more at the process of escaping from the snare of the fear of man, but for today it has just been good to look at the example of our Lord.

The early disciples hung around Jesus long enough and were filled with the Holy Spirit powerfully enough that they crossed that line, too. Peter and John fearlessly preached the gospel to the hostile Jewish leaders. After their arrest, this is how the biblical writer, Luke, summed up the leaders' reaction to the two prisoners:

> Now as they observed the confidence of Peter and
> John and understood that they were uneducated
> and untrained men, they were amazed, and began to
> recognize them as having been with Jesus.
>
> Acts 4:13

I find it hard to imagine a higher compliment.

A THOUGHT TO CHEW ON

Our happiness is not dependent upon other people's approval.

A TRUTH TO REMEMBER

"The fear of man brings a snare, but he who trusts in the LORD will be exalted" (Proverbs 29:25).

A QUESTION TO MULL OVER

Are there people in your life whose approval you dread losing? Ask the Lord to show you why those relationships have such a hold on you.

TALKING IT OVER WITH GOD

Dear heavenly Father, one thing that is really obvious from the life of Your Son is that He fearlessly did right and said what needed to be said, no matter who He was with. It also eventually got Him killed, which isn't really encouraging. I guess ultimately being free from the fear of man comes on the heels of being free from the fear of death, doesn't it?

Thank You that You are in the process of making me like Jesus. What that will ultimately involve remains to be seen, but as I look at what His followers in the Bible went through then as well as what many of them in various parts of the world go through now, there is a cost to living above the fear of man. I'm not going to worry about that, because I know that Your grace is sufficient for anything You call me to go through.

Please make me courageous, Lord. Make me like Jesus. No matter what it takes, no matter what it costs, that is what I want more than anything else. Somehow I sense that resolve will be tested somewhere down the road. I trust Your grace to enable me to truly step over that invisible line... and stay there. Amen.

Day 28: God's Got Your Back

Jesus could be very blunt at times. It comes with the territory of being courageous and not fearing people. But Jesus was only blunt when bluntness was called for. This was one of those times.

He was preparing His twelve disciples for their first mission trip without Him. There were lots of helpful instructions from Jesus regarding what to take, where to stay, as well as what exciting things awaited them in terms of ministry. Jesus also spared no words in warning them about the trials that they would encounter. He let them know in no uncertain terms that the tough times He went through, they would experience also.

It was almost like the final words of a battle-tested general before sending his troops out on a crucial mission. I'm sure the men were hanging on every word of Jesus, at some level scared and at another level chomping at the bit to bravely face what awaited them.

No, it would not be all fun and games. There was risk. There was danger. But in their greatest moments of peril, they could count on the Father's Spirit to give them just the right words to say.

As Jesus warned His men about the persecution they would experience, He could read the fear in their eyes. And so His words were blunt:

> Therefore do not fear them, for there is nothing
> concealed that will not be revealed, or hidden that will
> not be known. What I tell you in the darkness, speak
> in the light; and what you hear whispered in your ear,
> proclaim upon the housetops. Do not fear those who kill
> the body but are unable to kill the soul; but rather fear
> Him who is able to destroy both soul and body in hell.

Matthew 10:26–28

Now, I've got to be perfectly honest with you. At first glance, I'm not sure how encouraged I would have been had I been one of the twelve disciples.

First of all, I would not have been too thrilled to be reminded that the people I was going to minister to might decide to repay my kindness to them by killing me.

Second, I would *really* not be thrilled to be reminded that the God whom I was about to serve could do a lot worse. He could toss me into the fires of hell if He so chose.

If you've ever read these verses in Matthew before, you were probably like me... you hurried over them and tried to dispel the uneasiness they caused. But let's take a closer look at them and see how Jesus actually used them to encourage the hearts of His disciples and how He wants to use them to provide us with the grace to not fear people.

The first thing we need to observe is that the main point Jesus was making was to not be afraid of what man can do. That's very relevant for all of us, even if we don't happen to live in a place where it's risky to share our faith. Throughout the Bible it's clear God wants to set us free from the fear of man. Check out Psalm 56:1–4:

> Be gracious to me, O God, for man has trampled upon me;
> Fighting all day long he oppresses me.
> My foes have trampled upon me all day long,
> For they are many who fight proudly against me.
> When I am afraid,
> I will put my trust in You.
> In God, whose word I praise,
> in God I have put my trust;
> I shall not be afraid.
> What can mere man do to me?

The last question King David asks in that passage might seem a bit strange to you. I mean, in just those four verses he uses terms like "trampled upon," "fighting all day long," "oppresses," "fighting proudly against me." It's obvious that men could and did do lots of things to David. They could even have killed him. He realized that.

But notice David's point: he was not going to let the fear of what people could do control him, because He knew God was in control. So he chose to put his trust in the Lord and in His word. He knew God had his back, and if for some reason the Lord allowed harm or even death to come to David, he would still trust in God and not be afraid.

You see, being free from the fear of man doesn't guarantee that nothing bad will ever happen to you at the hands of men. It just means you are choosing to put your trust in the Lord to take care of you and you're not going to live your life controlled by the fear of people… but by faith in God.

That's really the point that Jesus was making. In essence He was saying, "Sure, men can kill you, but they can't do a thing to touch the *real* you… your soul. So don't be afraid of people and what they can do to your physical body. Trust God. This earthly tent is going to die and turn back to dust anyway. The real you is safe."

Let's put what Jesus said into the context of our antidote to fear, which is to remove one of the fear object's two attributes – its *presence* or its *power*. Jesus doesn't try and remove the *presence* of people. After all, as the salt of the earth and the light of the world (Matthew 5:13–16), we're called to a world of people to bring them the good news. That was what Jesus was preparing them for in Matthew 10 anyway… to engage humanity, not hide from it.

So Jesus was seeking to remove the *power* of the fear of man from the hearts and minds of His disciples by putting the worst that man can do into its proper context. "Yeah, so they can kill your body. So what? Your soul – the real you – lives on."

So, you might be asking, what about that part in Matthew 10 about fearing the One who can destroy your body and soul in hell? What was that all about?

First of all, Jesus knew His disciples. He knew that God had chosen them as His followers and that they would take the good news to the world and one day join Him in heaven. So Jesus wasn't threatening them with hell... with the possible exception of Judas Iscariot. It is possible that this warning was meant at some level for him, for Jesus knew he was a false disciple. But Jesus, knowing those that were His own, was clearly not threatening the other 11 with the prospect of their going to hell.

So what was Jesus doing? First, I think He was simply making the point that the fear of God trumps the fear of man. God has much more power than men, so if you fear people and not God, you've got it backwards.

Second, Jesus certainly could have been emphasizing the almost unfathomable importance of their mission. They were going out to bring good news to people who were indeed in danger of going to hell without Christ. Therefore, the proper perspective for the disciples would be not to worry about themselves (for the worst that could happen to them would be to die physically), but to worry about those they were going out to bring the gospel to (for the worst that could happen to them was far worse).

Finally, just in case you remain unconvinced of Jesus' loving, gracious heart toward His disciples, take a look at His words in Matthew 10:29–31, the ones He spoke immediately after the passage we quoted earlier:

Are not two sparrows sold for a cent? And yet not one of
them will fall to the ground apart from your Father. But
the very hairs of your head are all numbered. So do not
fear; you are more valuable than many sparrows.

Jesus said it to His disciples, and He says it to you and me,
three times in the same chapter of Matthew: *do not fear*. Our
Father loves us and will take care of us. Isn't it time to finally
say "no" to the fear of people that has held you back from
being yourself? Believe me, it feels great to be real... to be
yourself. And who are you? You are a precious, dearly loved
child of God called to be Christ's ambassador. Just like the
first disciples, Jesus wants to use you to take the good news to
those who are in grave danger without it. Will you trust God
to take care of you?

Who is there to harm you if you prove zealous for what
is good? But even if you should suffer for the sake of
righteousness, you are blessed. And do not fear their
intimidation, and do not be troubled, but sanctify Christ
as Lord in your hearts, always being ready to make a
defense to everyone who asks you to give an account
for the hope that is in you, yet with gentleness and
reverence...

1 Peter 3:13–15

A THOUGHT TO CHEW ON

When you stop fearing people, you are finally free to truly be
yourself.

A TRUTH TO REMEMBER

"Who is there to harm you if you prove zealous for what is
good?" (1 Peter 3:13).

A QUESTION TO MULL OVER

Who are the people in your world that need to hear about Jesus? How is the fear of man holding you back from telling them? How could Jesus' words in Matthew 10:26–28 help motivate you to reach out to them?

TALKING IT OVER WITH GOD

Dear heavenly Father, I am not afraid that if I don't tell people about You, I'll go to hell. Your grace has saved me as I have placed my faith in Jesus alone. But I am very concerned about my loved ones and friends who don't know You. They are in real danger. I won't bother making excuses for the times in the past where I have held back from boldly speaking about You out of fear. I thank You for Your complete forgiveness and cleansing from those sins of fearing man more than You.

Could I make a new start today, not by some "grit your teeth" determination on my part, but by Your grace? Please empower me by the same Holy Spirit that gave boldness to the early disciples. I ask for the courage to speak up when I need to, shut up when I should, and stand up when Your name, Your ways and Your word are opposed. After all, what can people do to me... really? You've got my back. Thanks, Lord. Amen.

The Power of Humility

Day 29: Grace Flows Downhill

Somebody has said that humility is the one character quality that the moment you think you've got it, you've lost it. Well, that may be true for us mere mortals, but it certainly wasn't the case for the Lord Jesus. Notice how He described Himself in one of His most famous invitations:

> Come to Me, all who are weary and heavy-laden, and I will give you rest. Take My yoke upon you and learn from Me, for I am gentle and humble in heart, and you will find rest for your souls. For My yoke is easy and My burden is light.
>
> Matthew 11:28–30

We'll talk more in-depth about this invitation next week, but for now I want you to focus on the two words that Jesus used to describe His character. As far as I know, this is the only place in the gospels where Jesus used adjectives to tell us what He's like. All the other times He used metaphors like, "I am the bread of life" (John 6:35), or "I am the good shepherd" (John 10:11), or "I am the true vine" (John 15:1) – that sort of thing.

But here, Jesus came right out and described Himself as "gentle" and "humble." Pretty amazing! Of all the words our Lord could have used, He chose these two. He had the chance to say, "… for I am God the Almighty, holy and perfect, all-knowing and eternal," and that would have been completely true. But instead He described Himself as *gentle* and *humble*.

And indeed He was… and is.

What image comes to your mind when you hear Jesus describe Himself as being "humble"? Does it make Him seem *mild-mannered* or *weak*? Does this humility repel you or attract you? Does it make Jesus appear *very vulnerable* and *unable* or maybe even *unwilling to protect or stand up for Himself*?

Would you like people to regard you as humble? If it were true, would you, like Jesus, readily identify yourself as being humble?

In this fifth week, we are going to turn our attention to the problem of pride and the need for humility. We'll look at what humility is. We'll discuss whether pride is always a negative quality. We'll examine what happens when pride rules. And we'll discover what results when humility reigns.

Whether it is humbling oneself before God or other people, God's grace is connected to humility. Two New Testament passages come immediately to mind:

> But He gives a greater grace. Therefore it says, "God is opposed to the proud, but gives grace to the humble." Submit therefore to God. Resist the devil and he will flee from you.
>
> James 4:6–7

> You younger men, likewise, be subject to your elders; and all of you, clothe yourselves with humility toward one another, for "God is opposed to the proud, but gives grace to the humble." Therefore, humble yourselves under the mighty hand of God, that He may exalt you at the proper time, casting all your anxiety on Him, because He cares for you. Be of sober spirit, be on the alert. Your adversary, the devil, prowls around like a roaring lion, seeking someone to devour. But resist him, firm in your faith…
>
> 1 Peter 5:5–9a

Clearly, pride is to be avoided (unless you happen to enjoy having God Himself oppose you!) and true humility is to be sought after. If pride means to exalt yourself (move yourself up) and humility means to exalt God and others (move yourself down), then you could say that pride is like a mountain and humility is like a valley. And God's grace is like water, and water always flows downward... into the valley of humility.

As we begin our journey to these valley lands, if we want to know what humility truly is, we need to start with Jesus, since He described Himself as humble. And He wasn't deceived or conceited when He said that. He was, as our British friends like to say, "spot on."

There are a couple of verses in the gospel of John that will help us begin to grasp humility, I think. In John 5:19 Jesus explained how He lived so that those who wanted to kill Him could understand:

> Therefore Jesus answered and was saying to them,
> "Truly, truly I say to you, the Son can do nothing of
> Himself, unless it is something He sees the Father doing;
> for whatever the Father does, these things the Son also
> does in like manner..."

And later on in that same chapter, Jesus said (verse 30):

> I can do nothing on My own initiative. As I hear, I judge;
> and My judgment is just, because I do not seek My own
> will, but the will of Him who sent Me.

Humility, therefore, should not be confused with *passivity*. Passivity is doing nothing. Humility is doing nothing on your own initiative, but seeking out, surrendering to and obeying the will of the One in charge, God the Father.

With this understanding of humility, you can see why God

would oppose the proud but give grace (favor) to the humble. God is always going to stand against those who stand against His will. How could He do otherwise? Conversely, it is clear that God will always support, encourage, and empower – in other words, give grace to – those who are in alignment with His will and purposes.

Let's get another view of the humility of Jesus from Philippians 2:3–8:

> Do nothing from selfishness or empty conceit, but with humility of mind, regard one another as more important than yourselves; do not merely look out for your own personal interests, but also for the interests of others. Have this attitude in yourselves which was also in Christ Jesus, who, although He existed in the form of God, did not regard equality with God a thing to be grasped, but emptied Himself, taking the form of a bond-servant, and being made in the likeness of men. Being found in appearance as a man, He humbled Himself by becoming obedient to the point of death, even death on a cross.

Humility is evidenced by the deep desire to make sure others are taken care of, while not worrying about whether you are noticed or rewarded. In its purest form, humility is the willingness to serve others in love for their good, even to the loss of one's reputation... or life. The supreme example of this was Jesus Himself. He willingly left heaven and its glory to live as a Man (limited by time and space) on this planet, and to totally surrender Himself to the Father's will, even allowing the people He created to reject and crucify Him, so that we could be rescued from our darkness.

It is, I believe, beyond our ability to understand such a lowering of oneself that Jesus demonstrated, and yet stunningly we are told to have that same attitude in ourselves. If ever we needed God's grace, it is here, because developing humility is not engineered by the will of man but by a work of God.

Society says to "look out for number one." Actually that's very good advice, just so long as you remember who Number One actually is! And, by the way, when you look out for God's and others' interests rather than your own, you find God taking quite good care of you when it is all said and done. Here's the rest of the story of Jesus' humility, found in Philippians 2:9–11:

> For this reason also, God highly exalted Him, and bestowed on Him the name which is above every name, so that at the name of Jesus every knee will bow, of those who are in heaven and on earth and under the earth, and that every tongue will confess that Jesus Christ is Lord, to the glory of God the Father.

A THOUGHT TO CHEW ON

Jesus is gentle and humble in heart.

A TRUTH TO REMEMBER

"Have this attitude in yourselves which was also in Christ Jesus…" (Philippians 2:5).

A QUESTION TO MULL OVER

On a scale of 1 to 10 (1 being *not at all* and 10 being *all the way*), where does the quality of "humility" fall on your personal character quality wish list? How important do you think humility is to God?

TALKING IT OVER WITH GOD

Dear Father, in some ways I sense that You are drilling deeper, the farther along in this devotional that we go. Dealing with guilt was important as I looked at the things I have done. I needed to know Your forgiveness and cleansing. Then came shame and fear where we took a look deeper down into the thoughts and motivations of my heart. I am so grateful for the new identity You are revealing to me and the courage You are building in me.

But somehow the subject of pride hits at the core, because it means You want to access areas where I am largely blind... things You see but I often can't. Thank You that You are gentle and humble in heart, so I trust the "earth mover" of Your Spirit to work carefully as I become more like Your Son. Please be patient with my defense mechanisms that offer resistance and don't stop Your work until every mountain in my life is made low and all the high places are demolished and turned into broad valleys where Your grace can freely flow. Amen.

Day 30: Is Pride Ever a Good Thing?

The question posed by today's title is an interesting one, as you'll see in a minute. Strictly speaking, however, the answer is *no*. Every time the word "pride" is used in the Bible, it is clearly referring to something that is evil. It represents man's attempt to live independently of God, thinking he's got it all under control, not needing anyone's help. It results in self-centeredness, which is the opposite of love, and can develop into an arrogant, judgmental or even cruel attitude of superiority to others, taking all the credit for the good that comes one's way and refusing to accept any of the blame. And God is very much opposed to it. King Solomon warned about pride when he wrote:

> Pride goes before destruction,
> And a haughty spirit before stumbling.
>
> Proverbs 16:18

Make no mistake about it, pride is evil, and since Jesus described Himself as "humble," to be proud is to be unlike Christ, even anti-Christ.

Before we spend the rest of the week facing the issue of destructive pride and sounding a clarion call for humility, I want to make sure to clarify something. There is something in life that in common language is often called "pride" (but isn't really), that actually is a positive quality. That is, there are times when it is good and appropriate to have a sense of joyful, personal satisfaction over something or someone.

First, Scripture indicates that it is OK to take personal satisfaction in what you have accomplished. That's what Galatians 6:2–5 says:

> Bear one another's burdens, and thereby fulfill the law
> of Christ. For if anyone thinks he is something when
> he is nothing, he deceives himself. But each one must
> examine his own work, and then he will have reason for
> boasting in regard to himself alone, and not in regard to
> another. For each one will bear his own load.

There's a lot of great stuff in these four verses.

First of all, we are to eagerly help others when they are weighed down by the crushing burdens of life. This is love and an expression of Christ's good will for us.

Second, it is easy to think too highly of ourselves. If we go around boasting about how great we are when, in fact, we've done nothing coming close to warranting that kind of boasting, we're just fooling ourselves. Everybody else will see that we're full of hot air; usually we're the last to know or realize it.

Third – and this is our main point here – if we in fact do well and our work is good, then it is right to feel a sense of personal satisfaction in what we've done. Somebody might say, "Hey, come take a look at the new cabinet I'm building. I'm pretty proud of it." What he's really meaning to say is that it brings him a lot of joy and satisfaction.

I might add, he would do well to remember that it is God who gives any of us the ability to do work well; that reminder helps keep us humble and protects us from pride. The caveat in this scripture is that our boasting should not be "in regard to another." In the case of the cabinet-maker, he is (hopefully) not really meaning, "And I'm better than you because you can't do this and I can!" That *would* be pride.

The Bible, in fact, warns us not to compare ourselves with others at all. It is either going to lead to pride or envy, depending on how you measure up… or don't measure up. Paul, in 2 Corinthians 10:12, discouraged this kind of behavior:

> For we are not bold to class or compare ourselves
> with some of those who commend themselves; but
> when they measure themselves by themselves and
> compare themselves with themselves, they are without
> understanding.

Second, the Bible says that it is very appropriate to find personal satisfaction and joy in the character development and accomplishments of others. Paul apparently boasted to Titus about how warm and encouraging the folks in the church of Corinth were. Listen to Paul's words from 2 Corinthians 7:13b, 14:

> And besides our comfort, we rejoiced even much more
> for the joy of Titus, because his spirit has been refreshed
> by you all. For if in anything I have boasted to him
> about you, I was not put to shame; but as we spoke all
> things to you in truth, so also our boasting before Titus
> proved to be the truth.

Earlier in that same letter, the apostle wrote:

> Great is my confidence in you; great is my boasting on
> your behalf. I am filled with comfort; I am overflowing
> with joy in all our affliction.
>
> 2 Corinthians 7:4

Someone might say in today's vernacular, "Ah, Paul was really proud of the Corinthians." Well, not exactly. He didn't regard them as superior to other churches nor did he play favorites. He was, however, genuinely filled with joy over their progress in the faith. You also get the strong sense that the Thessalonian church was Paul's "pride and joy," as he rejoiced over their growth in faith, hope and love (see particularly 1 Thessalonians 2:19–20). Yes, it is normal and healthy to find personal joy and satisfaction in the successes of those we love... especially those into whose lives we have personally invested.

As I think back over my kids' lives, there are many moments of deep satisfaction and joy in watching them grow up. Getting to see them stagger across the room, taking their first steps as toddlers. Seeing the brightness in their eyes and excitement on their faces as they prepared to start kindergarten. Watching them overcome fears and learn to ride a bicycle. Shouting with delight when they made a good play on the athletic field. Standing with tears as they received their high school diplomas. Being there when they opened their hearts to Jesus. Listening to them teach me what the Lord has taught them. Dropping them off at college, knowing they were ready for that next big step. Life is filled with moments of deep joy and satisfaction like this, and they are good gifts from God.

This isn't really the main point of this devotional, but the thought just occurred to me: *Have you ever realized that God the Father was beaming with deep satisfaction and joy over you when you took these steps of faith in your life?* He was... and is. Maybe you needed to know that today.

Finally, there is a *third* way in which this deep satisfaction and joy shows up: It is healthy and holy to boast in the Lord Himself. To boast in the Lord is right and good and is actually a very smart way to protect oneself from the wrong kind of prideful boasting. After all, if you spend all your time thinking about and telling other people how great God is, you'll not have any time (or desire, for that matter) to brag about yourself!

We ought to, in a sense, be "proud of" (as opposed to being ashamed of!) our Lord, for He is truly amazing. I love what Moses wrote in Exodus 15:11:

Who is like You among the gods, O Lᴏʀᴅ?
Who is like You, majestic in holiness,
Awesome in praises, working wonders?

The theme of boasting comes up a lot in Paul's letters to the Corinthians, as we've already seen. Since boasting seemed to be such a big part of life in that city, the apostle decided to set them all straight, and encouraged them in the right kind of boasting. He wrote in 1 Corinthians 1:26–31:

For consider your calling, brethren, that there were not
many wise according to the flesh, not many mighty, not
many noble; but God has chosen the foolish things of
the world to shame the wise, and God has chosen the
weak things of the world to shame the things which are
strong, and the base things of the world and the despised
God has chosen, the things that are not, so that He may
nullify the things that are, so that no man may boast
before God. But by His doing you are in Christ Jesus,
who became to us wisdom from God, and righteousness
and sanctification, and redemption, so that, just as it is
written, "Let him who boasts, boast in the Lᴏʀᴅ."

People brag about and show off all the craziest things... from their abs to their favorite sports teams and memorabilia to their new clothes to their old homes... ad nauseam. But if we are going to boast and brag about something, why not boast and brag about the Best – the Lord Himself! We'll close today with Jeremiah's wise counsel:

Thus says the Lᴏʀᴅ, "Let not a wise man boast of his
wisdom, and let not the mighty man boast of his might,
let not a rich man boast of his riches; but let him who
boasts boast of this, that he understands and knows
Me, that I am the Lᴏʀᴅ who exercises lovingkindness,

justice and righteousness on earth; for I delight in these things," declares the LORD.

Jeremiah 9:23–24

A THOUGHT TO CHEW ON

It is normal and healthy to take great satisfaction and joy and even boast in the successes of those we love.

A TRUTH TO REMEMBER

"Let him who boasts, boast in the LORD" (1 Corinthians 1:31).

A QUESTION TO MULL OVER

If someone were to attach a microphone to you and record your words for a week, what would that recording reveal about what or who you boast or brag about? We talk about what is most important to us. What or who is most important to you? Why?

TALKING IT OVER WITH GOD

Dear Father, I think it must be human nature to talk about and even boast about the things that are most important to us. It is freeing to know that it's OK to You that I take pleasure and satisfaction in a job well done. It also makes all the sense in the world that You would smile when I take personal joy and satisfaction in the successes of my loved ones, because You delight in my steps of faith. Keep me, please, from pride and the foolish notion that I am somehow better than others because of anything that I have done. All that I have accomplished, You have done for me (Isaiah 26:12b).

Therefore, I want to boast with all my might in who You are. I want the spotlight to be where it belongs... on

You! You are truly amazing and if I would boast about anything about myself, let it be that I have been given the unbelievable privilege of knowing You as the God of lovingkindness, righteousness and justice. Amen.

Day 31: My Will or Thy Will?

Every person on planet earth and especially every child of God is a player in a cosmic drama… a participant in a war of the worlds. It is an unseen war, an invisible battle that most people are largely unaware of, and yet it is of far greater consequence than any we might see depicted on the evening news. It is a war between God and Satan; good and evil; the Kingdom of Light versus the domain of darkness.

Unlike other wars, the outcome of this war is not in question. Jesus wins. Satan loses. End of story.

But before you pack up your armor and put it away for good in the attic, you need to realize something. Yes, the war is won, but the battles are not over. Though the end is sure, the end has not yet come. There are very significant battles and skirmishes being fought all across the world every day. Nations, races of people, universities, denominations, churches, families and individual lives still hang in the balance. Which side will they end up on?

You and I are soldiers in this battle whether we like it or not. The question is not whether we will be in the war. The question is which side will we choose and what kind of impact will we make?

Since you have made it this far in this devotional, it is probably fair to assume you have chosen the Kingdom of Light. If you haven't made that clear-cut choice yet, it's not too late, but I wouldn't wait. To have received thirty days of light and still not responded to Jesus, the Light of the world, is very dangerous. The darkness may have more of a hold on you than you think. Paul wrote in Ephesians 5:6–10:

> Let no one deceive you with empty words, for because
> of these things the wrath of God comes upon the sons of

disobedience. Therefore do not be partakers with them; for you were formerly darkness, but now you are Light in the Lord; walk as children of Light (for the fruit of the Light consists in all goodness and righteousness and truth), trying to learn what is pleasing to the Lord.

The title of today's devotional gives a clue as to the "mottoes" of these two kingdoms. The domain of darkness says, "My will be done." The Kingdom of Light says (referring to God), "Thy will be done." The distinction is profound.

The original light-bearer, an archangel named Lucifer, made a huge mistake. One day he must have been looking in a mirror, saying, "Mirror, mirror on the wall, who's the fairest of them all?" The answer was God, but that wasn't the answer Lucifer – who then became Satan, the prince of darkness – wanted to hear. Listen to his heart of pride:

> But you said in your heart,
> "I will ascend to heaven;
> I will raise my throne above the stars of God,
> And I will sit on the mount of assembly
> In the recesses of the north.
> I will ascend above the heights of the clouds;
> I will make myself like the Most High."
>
> Isaiah 14:13–14

Talk about pride! Of course Lucifer-turned-Satan never saw his "I wills" fulfilled, but he still is doing everything he can to undermine the Kingdom of Light. And he is actively recruiting those who will live by his creed of "My will be done."

Contrast this picture with the Lord Jesus in the Garden of Gethsemane as He pondered going to the cross to bear the sins of the entire world:

And He took with Him Peter and the two sons of
Zebedee, and began to be grieved and distressed. Then
He said to them, "My soul is deeply grieved, to the
point of death; remain here and keep watch with Me."

And He went a little beyond them, and fell on His
face and prayed, saying, "My Father, if it is possible,
let this cup pass from Me; yet not as I will, but as You
will"…

He went away again a second time and prayed,
saying, "My Father, if this cannot pass away unless I
drink it, Your will be done"… And He left them again,
and went away and prayed a third time, saying the
same thing once more.

Matthew 26:37–44

While the disciples slept, Jesus agonized. And though He
struggled with His decision whether to go to the cross, in the
end He surrendered and prayed, "Thy will be done." Jesus
drank the cup and suffered and died. And the rest is His story.

The humility of Jesus versus the pride of Satan. The Lamb
slain versus the lion roaring. The Lamb wins, as do all that
follow Him in humility. The roaring lion loses, as do all who
follow him in pride.

The problem with pride is that it's kind of like bad
breath… you're likely going to be the last one to know you
have it and very rarely will anybody tell you. But keep your
ears open. People may use other words to describe you that
are telltale signs that pride, and not humility, is reigning in
your life. Words like:

- Stubborn
- Impatient
- Never listen
- Inflexible
- Controller

- Set in your ways
- Condescending
- Independent
- Vain
- Diva/prima donna
- Self-sufficient
- Spoiled
- Limelighter
- Judgmental
- Critical
- Cruel.

Sometimes we bear these labels with… well… *pride*. We consider them compliments. They are not. Other times we deny them, thinking people just don't understand us. And maybe they don't. But God does, and that is not how He wants us to be.

Contrast those descriptions with Colossians 3:12–14:

> So, as those who have been chosen of God, holy and beloved, put on a heart of compassion, kindness, humility, gentleness and patience; bearing with one another, and forgiving each other, whoever has a complaint against anyone; just as the Lord forgave you, so also should you. Beyond all these things put on love, which is the perfect bond of unity.

God's grace, His favor, His enabling power is given to the humble, James 4:6 says. And 1 Peter 5:12 tells us to stand firm in that grace. When we do, humility reigns and the darkness is pushed back and the Light shines brighter. And love wins.

When we choose to walk in pride, the darkness closes in. The darkness divides. And the darkness devours.

"My will" or "Thy will." Which will, will you choose?

A THOUGHT TO CHEW ON

Light flourishes in humility. Darkness feeds on pride.

A TRUTH TO REMEMBER

"… yet not as I will, but as You will" (Matthew 26:39b).

A QUESTION TO MULL OVER

Surrender of our will to God does not come easily to any of us. Why do you think that is? How does knowing God as a God of great grace, love, mercy, power and faithfulness help in making the decision to choose humility?

TALKING IT OVER WITH GOD

Dear Father of Light, there is no darkness in You at all. You know, better than I, that so much of this world in which I live is enveloped in darkness. In fact, the whole world lies in the power of the evil one (1 John 5:19). It is easy to feel overwhelmed and outnumbered. But thank You that Jesus, the Light of the world, has triumphed and the darkness could neither comprehend nor overwhelm Him (John 1:5).

Please remind me that I'm on the winning side when the world makes me feel like a loser and when the world broadcasts the message that surrender to You is feeble and weak and that only the strong and self-reliant survive. I renounce proud self-sufficiency and I choose humility and dependence upon You. And I can wait for the rewards and the accolades. Those who choose pride may get them now, but they will lose them. Those who choose humility will have them one day, forever. Amen.

Day 32: The Litmus Test

How can you tell if you are doing well spiritually? That's a really intriguing question, and how you answer it will reveal a lot about how well you know and understand God and His grace. Before tackling that question, however, we need to take a look at a bigger issue.

I think it is pretty much human nature to somehow try and turn things that are meant to be immaterial into things that are concrete. To reduce the intangible and mysterious into things that we can see, hear, taste, touch and smell. Personally, I think that's a large part of the problem with idols. Do you remember the first and second commandments?

> I am the LORD your God, who brought you out of the land of Egypt, out of the house of slavery.
>   You shall have no other gods before Me.
>   You shall not make for yourself an idol, or any likeness of what is in heaven above or on the earth beneath or in the water under the earth. You shall not worship them or serve them; for I, the LORD your God, am a jealous God…
>
> Exodus 20:2–5a

As you might recall, as Moses was finishing up his forty-day spiritual retreat on top of Mount Sinai, the rank and file were doing something rank and vile down in the valley… in direct violation of those commandments. Under Moses' brother's leadership, they were making the infamous golden calf. Listen to how Aaron described that piece of metal:

> This is your god, O Israel, who brought you up from the land of Egypt.
>
> Exodus 32:4b

This unsacred cow was a big hit with the people. They were much happier with a god they could control and which did not bother them with frightening words and thunder, lightning and trumpet blasts. They were so happy they decided to throw an orgy in celebration, though Aaron tried unsuccessfully to redeem it, calling it "a feast to the LORD," complete with burnt offerings and peace offerings (see Exodus 32:5–6).

Somehow the Lord wasn't in a partying mood and neither was Moses when he came down off his mountaintop experience. He made the people grind the despicable idol into dust and drink it for breakfast.

Idols are hideous because nothing that is made of this earth can even remotely represent the infinite, holy Creator. And for human hands to make something and then to declare it to be "god," and especially "God," has to be about as sickening to the Lord of glory as can be imagined. But that's precisely what the people did and it's exactly what hundreds of millions of people around the world do today. Even followers of Christ can be guilty of idolatry.

"God is spirit," Jesus told us in John 4:24, "and those who worship Him must worship in spirit and truth." Idolatry is trying to worship God in "body" (as opposed to "spirit"), and in so doing, ending up worshipping Him in lies rather than truth. At its core, idolatry is making "God" into our own image. Rather than worshipping and serving the God who is, we are duped into forming and following a "God" that is not.

So what does all of this have to do with trying to figure out how well we are doing spiritually? A lot, actually.

Just as we can try and remake God into something tangible, that we can wrap our minds and hands around... so we can do with the Christian life. The human side of us (apart from Christ), which is called "flesh" in the Bible, likes to control; and to control something we tend to analyze, quantify and even create a formula for it. It is easy to come up with a way to analyze, quantify and even create a formula to determine how well we are doing spiritually.

And it is also very easy to think that God approves of or is even the author of our formulaic Christianity. We view Him as a sort of heavenly Santa Claus who is "making a list and checking it twice." He's "going to find out who's naughty and nice." We perceive Him as having some kind of religious "to do" and "to don't" list. And in our imagination, He checks things off about us on a daily basis, evaluating whether we are good or bad boys or girls.

If we believe we are faithfully following the formula, we think we are doing well; if we perceive ourselves as falling short, we tend to view ourselves as failures. The first situation breeds pride; the second guilt, shame and maybe envy. All are wrong.

To believe that God relates to us on the basis of those kinds of "works of the Law" is... well... a *dis*grace.

What are your litmus tests for spirituality? Here are some of the more common ones:

- Daily Bible reading
- Daily prayers
- Weekly (if not more often) church attendance
- Busy service in the church
- Respect from others in the church
- A ministry title or position
- Regularity in sharing your faith
- Faithful giving.

I remember so clearly when I was experiencing my early growing pains in the faith, that it was drilled into my head that in order to be spiritual I had to have a "quiet time." So I would dutifully make sure I spent some time each day to read my Bible and pray. Anything wrong with that? Of course not! There's a lot *right* with it, actually, since these are two of the means for us to grow in our love and trust of God.

The problem started when I began to gauge my relationship with God solely on the basis of whether I had my quiet time that day or not. If I did, I thought I was sure to receive God's blessings for the day; if I didn't, I expected my day to implode. So usually I made sure to have my quiet time! Who wouldn't?

Take a look back at the list above. Is there anything wrong with any of those things in the list? No, in fact many of those things are what growing, maturing Christians do. So what's the point?

The point is that our progress and well-being in the faith are not measured by the things we do but by the kind of people we are. Not by our outward performance of religious activity, but by our inner character of Christlikeness. Paul wrote:

> If I speak with the tongues of men and of angels, but do not have love, I have become a noisy gong or a clanging cymbal. If I have the gift of prophecy, and know all mysteries and all knowledge; and if I have all faith, so as to remove mountains, but do not have love, I am nothing. And if I give all my possessions to feed the poor, and if I deliver my body to be burned, but do not have love, it profits me nothing.
>
> 1 Corinthians 13:1–3

Those are familiar words, I expect, but no less poignant or profound despite their familiarity.

Love is what matters to God... loving Him, loving people. Having a heart that truly loves God will result in acts of devoted obedience to Him. Having a heart that truly loves people will result in acts of caring service to them. So if you are growing in your love for God and people and the qualities of love (see 1 Corinthians 13:4–8) are growing stronger in you as the days go by, you can know that, by His grace, you are doing well spiritually.

The spiritual activities listed earlier in today's devotional were never meant to be the "end" but rather expressions of the end, which is love. So yes, by all means, read the Bible and pray and go to church and share your faith, but in God's grace you'll find that you *want* to do those things to express His love, not feel like you *have* to do them out of fear of losing His love. Just remember, God doesn't love you more if you do (He already loves you as much as He ever will!); and don't think God loves you less if you don't (He does not change!).

God relates to us by grace, not by our works. We are accepted in Christ… period.

So where is the place for pride? Paul hit the nail on the head when he wrote:

> For who regards you as superior? What do you have
> that you did not receive? And if you did receive it, why
> do you boast as if you had not received it?
>
> 1 Corinthians 4:7

There's no room for pride when we see things as they really are. Our very life, breath, and heartbeat are things God gives us. The energy to get up in the morning, the strength to open your Bible, the wisdom to understand it, the power to tell others about Christ, the health to make it to church, the courage to do what's right… these things and many more are all things we have received as a gift of God's grace. Not one of them have we produced on our own.

When you truly grasp this, you are not filled with pride. You are filled with gratitude.

A THOUGHT TO CHEW ON

Your spiritual well-being is a matter of character, not performance.

A TRUTH TO REMEMBER

"What do you have that you did not receive?" (1 Corinthians 4:7b).

A QUESTION TO MULL OVER

In what way(s) do you try and quantify your spiritual well-being? How can these things become a source of pride, guilt, shame or envy?

TALKING IT OVER WITH GOD

Holy Lord and Father, You are immortal, invisible, the only wise God. To You and You alone belong all blessing and honor and glory forever. Please forgive me for the times I have created a picture of You in my mind that was not honoring to You. I know I have had the tendency to try and make You into a god that was controllable and predictable and out of that false picture, I have at times derived a formulaic view of my faith. I have many times tried to relate to You as a God who accepts or rejects me based on my performance as opposed to the God of grace that You are. I have also found myself lifted up in pride when I thought I was performing well or beaten down by guilt and shame or driven by envy when I wasn't.

To know that loving You and loving people in truth is what really matters to You makes things so much simpler. But, I also realize that actually being that kind of person – like Christ – is the hardest thing in the world to accomplish, as my self-centeredness runs pretty deep. So I see my need for Your grace even more. Thank You that You give a greater grace, which is exactly what I need. Amen.

Day 33: Cooperation or Competition?

As I am working at my dining room table, I have a really nice view out our back glass door, looking westward toward some of the Smoky Mountains. It is a beautiful, peaceful view and one that Shirley, the kids and I never take for granted.

Just outside the glass doors, dangling from the roof overhang is another, much closer view. It's a view of a hummingbird feeder. Red being the color of choice for hummingbirds, the feeder is basically red. The sweet liquid filling the glass globe is red. The pretend flowers into which the birds jam their hungry bills are red. There are some other red flowers painted on the feeder, too.

The closer view is not nearly as peaceful… especially this morning. At times there have been two and sometimes three hummingbirds vying for drinking rights at the feeder. Though there are four of the "flowers" where they can drink from and plenty of liquid for all, the little busybodies are not predisposed to share. Everything is fine when just one of them is at the feeder, but bring in two or more and feathers start to get ruffled.

In fact, in their furious flying, darting, jabbing at each other and driving one another off, they end up totally ignoring the reason for which they came to the feeder in the first place… to get nourishment!

On the continuum between cooperation and competition, they are off the charts on the competition side.

Since this is a devotional about our relationship to God and each other in grace, and since this week is about pride and humility, you can probably see where this is going.

But before we leave the world of hummingbirds and move on to how pride and humility affect the Church, there's something else of interest about these feathered mini-helicopters. Not only are they all hummingbirds; they are all of the same species of hummingbird. There is nothing particularly striking about them, by the way… they are kind of gray colored, humdrum really. But it wouldn't surprise me in the least if some of them are from the same nest or at least have a recent, common ancestor.

OK, now you *really* know where this is going. So be it. But before you toss this book down and pick up today's newspaper, let's look at a scripture that has a lot to say about the matter of cooperation versus competition. It is found in Ephesians 4:1–7:

> Therefore I, the prisoner of the Lord, implore you to walk in a manner worthy of the calling with which you have been called, with all humility and gentleness, with patience, showing tolerance for one another in love, being diligent to preserve the unity of the Spirit in the bond of peace. There is one body and one Spirit, just as also you were called in one hope of your calling; one Lord, one faith, one baptism, one God and Father of all who is over all and through all and in all.
>
> But to each one grace was given according to the measure of Christ's gift.

The first thing that jumps out at you when you read this scripture is that we have a lot more in common with other members of the body of Christ than we have in contrast. The commonalities are the major, important things. The differences are therefore minor. Why then do we so often focus on the differences and sweat the small stuff?

The fact that Christians of different church preferences have so much in common makes the spirit of competition so ridiculous and perplexing to non-believers. It is illustrated poignantly by the hummingbirds. They all look alike and could be brothers and sisters, for heaven's sake! I could see them cooperating together to fend off wasps or hornets or other things that would take their food and perhaps injure them, but what takes place at the feeder is a family feud.

The second thing of importance to notice from this scripture is that the first quality necessary for cooperation (unity) in the body of Christ is, guess what? That's right. Humility. Did you happen to notice the second quality? Gentleness. Didn't Jesus describe Himself as "gentle and humble" in heart (Matthew 11:28–30)? Living in cooperative unity requires the filling with the Spirit of the indwelling Christ, so that we are gentle and humble like Him.

What would happen if the Methodists thought the Baptists were more important than themselves, and the Baptists agreed... just kidding! What would happen if the Baptists went out of their way to put the Methodists first? And if the evangelicals sought to honor the charismatics who sought to honor the Pentecostals who sought to honor the Catholics and Orthodox and so on? What if angry, fearful, suspicious, proud, bitter competition or even just busyness within churches and apathy between churches were replaced by genuine, heartfelt humility and love resulting in unified cooperation?

The third thing we should notice from Ephesians 4 is that the apostle Paul implores – urgently, earnestly encourages – the believers to walk in unity. It is the only way that we followers of Christ can walk in a manner worthy of our calling. To be dis-unified in pride and a critical, harsh or fearful, separatist spirit is unworthy of Jesus and His calling of us as His body.

The fourth thing I notice is that we are not exhorted to *create* unity, but to *preserve* it. It's already there. It's already ours... in Christ! True, verses 8–11 talk about our differences, and that's necessary because the body of Christ is a *unity of diversity* not a *unity of conformity*. But the differences the Bible talks about are in the area of spiritual gifts and callings and roles within the body, not in denominational or doctrinal nuances.

Finally, what would happen if God's people truly believed that "to each one [of us] grace was given according to the measure of Christ's gift" (verse 7)? We would realize that we actually need each other and that when we are cut off from one member of the body, to that extent the body is diminished in its powerful impact.

We'll take a look tomorrow at what humble, loving unity demonstrated by cooperation in the body of Christ produces. It's called community.

A THOUGHT TO CHEW ON

Preserving unity in the body of Christ requires humility and gentleness.

A TRUTH TO REMEMBER

"But to each one [of us] grace was given according to the measure of Christ's gift" (Ephesians 4:7).

A QUESTION TO MULL OVER

In what ways do you view yourself or your church as superior to other Christians? Do you make an effort to cooperate with members of other denominations? Why or why not?

TALKING IT OVER WITH GOD

Dear heavenly Father, Creator of both hummingbirds and humans, You are the Lord of the universe, the Lord of the Church and the Lord of my life. Sin has deeply affected all of Your creation, hasn't it? And yet You have begun to reverse the curse that the first Adam brought, by sending the Last Adam to redeem lost humanity. You have adopted us all as Your sons and daughters and granted us all Your grace. You now have laid a crucial responsibility in our laps... to be diligent to preserve the unity that You have created in Christ.

Forgive us, Lord and forgive me, Lord, for we have done a terrible job with that calling. Instead of humility, we have walked in pride. Instead of gentleness, we have been critical, judgmental, suspicious and fearful. Instead of cooperating, we have competed against each other... even at times viewing others as the enemy. Meanwhile the real Enemy is delighted.

I repent of my selfish pride and ask the Spirit of Christ to build genuine humility in my soul and in Your body so that we would make an impact of love on a broken world. Amen.

Day 34: Real Community

I have the privilege of working with a ministry at church that is about the closest thing to real community that I've seen in a long, long while… maybe ever. There are no prima donnas in this gathering. The folks that are a part of this group are basic, down-to-earth people… both men and women. One is a machinist, another a printer, a couple others are nurses, one is a chiropractor, another is a real estate agent, still another works in hospital maintenance, and one is a retiree. There are others who have just become involved, so I'm not sure what line of work they are in. One thing I am sure of is that I'm the only one that is in full-time vocational ministry and I try not to let that interfere.

In fact, my desire has never been to be the one the community looks to for day-to-day leadership. Instead I have tried to provide some direction and encourage the others to minister to one another, to see leadership develop from within the ranks. Having a "professional minister" take over would have been really easy, but to be perfectly honest, it would have ruined it. So I stay in the background, helping rekindle vision and providing training when required, but the beauty of this community is that everyone is a minister. And it's fun to watch them begin to come to that realization.

Though this model may be significantly different from what you are used to, I suspect that what is happening in our midst is not all that far from what the Lord had in mind when He directed Paul to write Ephesians 4:11–13:

> And He gave some as apostles, and some as prophets,
> and some as evangelists, and some as pastors and
> teachers, for the equipping of the saints for the work
> of service, to the building up of the body of Christ;

until we all attain to the unity of the faith, and of the knowledge of the Son of God, to a mature man, to the measure of the stature which belongs to the fullness of Christ.

Did you catch that? The gifted ministers are not given by Christ to the body of Christ to do all the work. They are given to equip the saints to do the work! That is healthy community and that requires humility to function well. Those who are the equipping ministers eventually need to get out of the way and allow others to lead. Effective leaders eventually work themselves out of a job.

Another factor that creates an environment of life-giving humility is that everyone in the group has struggled with some kind of addiction or emotional dysfunction that at one time left them crippled in life. It's hard to fall into a "holier than thou" persona when you have felt like the scum of the earth.

On the other hand, it's impossible to wallow in self-pity (at least for long) when you have experienced the transforming grace of God… and you are part of a community of people who know who they are in Christ and who know who *you* are in Christ, and who aren't about to let you forget it!

Those that have remained in the group (and there have been some that have left for a variety of reasons) have stayed because of two primary reasons, I believe.

First, all of them have, during the course of growing together, shared their stories and have discovered in others a shame-busting grace reinforcing the biblical reality that "therefore there is now no condemnation for those who are in Christ Jesus" (Romans 8:1). Sadly, there can be a lot of condemnation in the Church, but thankfully that is not the case here.

Second, those in the group can't bear the thought of *not* getting together. They have grown to love each other too much to leave. When we considered only meeting once a month rather than weekly (because some of the lay leaders were pretty wiped out), they took a few weeks to consider the idea and then unanimously vetoed it.

That love involves things like calling and calling and eventually going over to someone's house when the shame of sin is spawning an unhealthy isolation in that member. Or taking a brother's guns and ammo away from him to make sure his depression doesn't turn lethal. Or providing a used vehicle to a needy brother for just the cost of new tires. Or piling in a couple of cars and traveling four hours one way to visit one of our fallen members at a residential treatment center. Or weeping and praying for another who has recently discovered he has Parkinson's disease.

Seeing these kinds of healthy relationships flourish isn't easy. It requires tough love at times... valuing the well-being of the brother or sister above one's own personal comfort. It means encouraging one another to not give up or give in but to hang in there and grow up... words that may not initially be joyfully received. This tough love requires humility of another kind... a humility defined as "confidence properly placed in God" rather than in oneself. This humility in dependence upon God brings great boldness that can be a lifesaver for a fellow believer. Let's continue with what Paul had to say in Ephesians 4:14–17:

> As a result, we are no longer to be children, tossed
> here and there by waves and carried about by every
> wind of doctrine, by the trickery of men, by craftiness
> in deceitful scheming; but speaking the truth in love,
> we are to grow up in all aspects into Him who is the
> head, even Christ, from whom the whole body, being
> fitted and held together by what every joint supplies,
> according to the proper working of each individual part,

causes the growth of the body for the building up of
itself in love.

We absolutely need God and we desperately need each other.
It's easy for God's people to get battered by bad teaching,
especially when they are young in the faith. So God has given
us each other to speak the truth in love so that we don't stay
in the spiritual crib or cradle but grow into mature, loving
adults in Christ... together. And everybody has something to
contribute to the cause.

As you read today's devotional, do you find a yearning
for this kind of community of loving, humble unity growing
in your heart?

Unity in the body and the honoring of our diverse gifts in
a spirit of oneness is the difference between cooperation and
competition... between a strong body and a weak and flabby
one... between a Church that is healthy, mature, impacting
the world and one that is divided, immature, impotent and
dismissed by the world.

A THOUGHT TO CHEW ON

We absolutely need God and we desperately need one another.

A TRUTH TO REMEMBER

"But speaking the truth in love, we are to grow up in all aspects
into Him who is the head, even Christ" (Ephesians 4:15).

A QUESTION TO MULL OVER

Are you involved in a community of believers that is
characterized by humility, unity and speaking the truth in
love? If not, what do you need to do in order to discover or
develop this kind of healthy, healing community?

TALKING IT OVER WITH GOD

Dear Father, what is being talked about in today's devotional sounds a lot like "family" to me… at least the way I've always envisioned families could be and should be. I can clearly see how humility is so needed, because if we walk in pride we don't think we really need anybody else and we certainly won't be committed to relationships in a way that is healthy and healing. Please release me from that independent, self-sufficient pride that leads to isolation and disunity, and remind me, when I'm tempted to try and make life work on my own, that the only cell in a body that lives on its own is cancer.

I admit to my neediness for others and I also admit that there really is, deep down, a longing for community that You have placed within me. Please direct me into that place of grace and love with other brothers and sisters so that the world would know that You sent Jesus. Amen.

Day 35: Breaking the Back of Prejudice

Here's the riddle for the day: *What do a fish, a plant, a worm and a wind have in common?* Hmmm. Maybe you are thinking, well they are all objects you find in nature. That's true, but sorry… it's not the right answer, at least for this riddle. If you are a Bible scholar, you might recognize that they are all mentioned in the book of Jonah. If you figured that out, you are getting warmer, but you haven't quite got it yet. Let me help you. Take a look at the following scriptures and then see if you can come up with the right answer:

> And the LORD appointed a great fish to swallow Jonah, and Jonah was in the stomach of the fish three days and three nights.
>
> Jonah 1:17

> So the LORD God appointed a plant and it grew up over Jonah to be a shade over his head to deliver him from his discomfort. And Jonah was extremely happy about the plant.
>
> Jonah 4:6

> But God appointed a worm when dawn came the next day and it attacked the plant and it withered.
>
> Jonah 4:7

> When the sun came up God appointed a scorching east wind, and the sun beat down on Jonah's head so that he became faint and begged with all his soul to die, saying, "Death is better to me than life."
>
> Jonah 4:8

What these four objects have in common is that each was "appointed" by God for a mission in Jonah's life. The Lord used these four things to rescue, direct, provide, protect, comfort and chasten Jonah. It's very encouraging to know that even in the midst of our disobedience (and Jonah was initially headed in the exact opposite direction from where God was sending him), God still cares about us deeply and cares for us creatively. However, for the purposes of today's devotional, I want to focus on God's chastening work in Jonah's life.

It's helpful, I think, to look at the story of Jonah and examine what problem he had that God was zeroing in on. And I don't think God was primarily concerned that Jonah was a bit of a drama queen... even though his reaction to the scorching east wind was a little over the top!

It doesn't take a rocket scientist as you read the book of Jonah to see that the man hated the people of Nineveh. Jonah's hatred was not totally unjustified either, by the way. They were a nasty, cruel people who seemed to be particularly bent on inflicting misery on their enemies, including the Hebrews.

Funny thing, then, that God would "appoint" Jonah to be the missionary to bring the city of Nineveh a prophetic message that would lead to their repentance and the withholding of God's judgment of destruction on them. I guess the twenty-first-century equivalent would be for God to send an Orthodox Jew to preach a message of repentance in Tehran, Iran. In some ways, however, Jonah was as much the "mission field" as were the Ninevites. You might say God was multitasking. He was intent on saving the Ninevites from destruction and he was determined to save Jonah from his hatred in the process.

Sometimes I wonder how much of God's blessing is withheld because of the racial prejudice that still exists within the Church. You might think the prejudice that exists today between races and ethnic groups in our nations and around the world is unique to this day and age. Not so. There was a huge rift in race relations that was true in Jonah's day and which Jesus also came to deal a death blow to in the first century. Listen in on how Paul described God's solution to the great division between Jew and Gentile:

> But now in Christ Jesus you who formerly were far off have been brought near by the blood of Christ. For He Himself is our peace, who made both groups into one and broke down the barrier of the dividing wall, by abolishing in His flesh the enmity, which is the Law of commandments contained in ordinances, so that in Himself He might make the two into one new man, thus establishing peace, and might reconcile them both in one body to God through the cross, by it having put to death the enmity.
>
> Ephesians 2:13–16

The "new man" Paul talked about was the new creation and transformation in Christ of Jews and Gentiles into children of God. He took those who were enemies of each other and made them part of a new family. The cost wasn't cheap, however. It cost Jesus His life. God had enough of the hatred between the races, and it took the ultimate sacrifice of His Son to break the back of this prejudice.

Jesus' heart for unity in the body of Christ is evident in how He prayed in John 17:22–23:

> The glory which You have given Me I have given to them, that they may be one, just as We are one; I in them and You in Me, that they may be perfected in unity, so that the world may know that You sent Me, and loved them, even as You have loved Me.

I call this "the great yet-to-be-answered prayer of Jesus." He is still praying it, I believe, today, because it has yet to come to pass. You and I could be part of that answer to prayer, you know, if we lay aside our pride and prejudice, and embrace humility, love and unity.

God appointed a fish, a plant, a worm and a wind to teach Jonah that He had "compassion on Nineveh" (Jonah 4:11) and that Jonah should, too. What has God appointed in your life to destroy the dividing wall between you and others? Maybe you are estranged from your spouse or your kids or your parents. Perhaps there is division within your church between those who have certain spiritual gifts and those who don't. Do you want nothing to do with "that church" down the street or on the other side of town because their theology is different from yours or because your church and theirs had a nasty split sometime in the past? Maybe your heart is divided against brothers and sisters who back a different political party. Could it be that there is prejudice against those of other races or ethnic groups? We are often quick to deny these things, but God knows.

As we conclude this devotional's fifth week, what is God saying to you? Is it possible that God is calling you to repent of some bias or bigotry or prejudice or attitude of superiority, isolation or division from another member or part of the body of Christ? Could it be that your heart change from pride to humility and disunity to unity could somehow be used by God to show the world that the Father sent Jesus and that He loves His people as much as He loves His Son?

A THOUGHT TO CHEW ON

We can be an answer to Jesus' prayer if we lay aside pride and prejudice and choose humility, love and unity.

A TRUTH TO REMEMBER

"For He Himself is our peace, who made both groups into one and broke down the barrier of the dividing wall" (Ephesians 2:14).

A QUESTION TO MULL OVER

Is the Lord surfacing any prejudice in your heart toward individuals, churches, denominations, races or ethnic groups? Take time to listen to what He may want and need to bring to your mind in this regard.

TALKING IT OVER WITH GOD

Dear Father, Your word says that there will be people from every tribe and tongue and people and nation in heaven. You love them all and Jesus died for them all. Right now I'm not so sure I would be totally comfortable with a heaven like that. I have a feeling that my tendency would be to hang out with the group that looks most like me. Would You please show me if there is any hidden prejudice in my heart? The comments I've made, the jokes I've told, the names I've called people, the deep-seated resentments, the fears… all of that is open and laid bare before Your holy eyes.

I trust that You are very able and quite willing to root out any denominational, racial or ethnic superiority that I might have and to make me like the Lord Jesus in this area. Please make me an instrument of unity. I choose humility in Christ and renounce any and all prejudice that I have allowed into my heart. Take Your surgeon's knife, Lord, and go as deep as You need to. Amen.

The "Grace-Rest" Life

Day 36: The Invitation

That sounds really good, doesn't it? The "grace-rest" life, I mean. And if you have been living under the crushing burden of guilt, shame, fear and pride, it not only sounds good, it *is* good. It is life as life was meant to be lived. We'll spend these last five days looking at what the "grace-rest" life is and how we can come to experience it.

I'm sure Jesus had the full attention of His listeners who were worn down and burned out by religious "dos" and "don'ts" when He said to them:

> Come to Me, all who are weary and heavy-laden, and I will give you rest. Take My yoke upon you and learn from Me, for I am gentle and humble in heart, and you will find rest for your souls. For My yoke is easy and My burden is light.
>
> Matthew 11:28–30

There are several things about this "grace-rest" life that immediately jump out at you as you read Jesus' words from Matthew 11.

First, the invitation is to come to Jesus. Not to a set of rules, regulations, duties and obligations. Not to a list of "shoulds, musts and oughts." Not to a religious system. Not to anyone's demands or expectations of what a Christian should be or do. Not to a life of rigid, strict, fearful control. Not even to your own self-imposed perfectionistic standards of what "being a good person" looks like. Come to Jesus.

Second, responding to the invitation brings the promise of *rest*. When you come to Jesus, He freely, graciously gives rest. Everything that comes from man-made, rule-based religious systems just wears you out. Hebrews 4:9–10 gives us a clue of what that rest entails:

> So there remains a Sabbath rest for the people of God. For the one who has entered His rest has himself also rested from his works…

This "rest" for the people of God is not so much tied into one day each week of inactivity (though such a practice is not a bad idea at all if enjoyed in liberty rather than dutifully fulfilled out of obligation). It is more a way of life. It is – and this is crucial to understand – ceasing from striving to live life rightly and make life work in your own strength, but instead trusting the only One who ever lived life rightly to be your source of life, strength, love and wisdom.

You might want to read that last sentence over a few times, asking God to penetrate your heart with the revelation of its power. That truth will revolutionize and transform your life… if you truly believe it.

Maybe the following story will help you lay hold of what we are talking about in terms of the "grace-rest" life. Once you grasp it, I don't believe you'll ever want to go back to the old way of living.

> On a clear, starry night in February, I cried out in utter helplessness, "Lord, I can't do it!"
> Those were to be my last words before ending my life with the rope I had brought to work that night. A beam high above my bench, a noose, one step… and an end to this misery at last. Twenty years of striving to

keep the rules, trying to guide my family "in the law" had ended in failure… failure at every turn. In the end, even the veneer of "living the moral and godly life" had cracked and splintered as I resorted to escaping the pain of failure through addiction to pornography, while my wife suffered from depression and an anxiety disorder. My children had turned to the world. A son and daughter chose the "gay" lifestyle; my other two sons simply found more "life" in the world than in the church. So why am I alive, writing these words? A miracle… grace… Jesus. In response to my cry that night, like a whisper I clearly heard the words, "No, you can't – but I can."

That starry night I surrendered. There was simply no question of going back to the law once I had felt that weight lift off my shoulders. The rest was simply learning to abide in Christ. I began reading the entire Bible, drinking great draughts of grace as I read whole New Testament books. What joy! Each step has been gently prepared by the Lord. Not once have I had to strive, but I am learning to abide in Christ and take the steps He ordains. Over the past three years the Lord has led me into ministry to others in bondage, and in a divine irony, I was ordained to the ministry last year, sanctioned and free to preach grace – unadulterated grace – within the same body that once had added such heavy burdens that grace was lost and hope nearly gone.[8]

Now, you may not be planning on taking your life, but maybe you are on the verge of giving up. Maybe you have concluded that the Christian life works for others but not for you. Perhaps you have become convinced that there is just something inherently wrong with you that prohibits you from "getting it." You've been going through the motions of doing the right things, the things that "good Christians" are supposed to do, but there doesn't seem to be any real life or heartfelt relational connection with God in them anymore. You wonder what's wrong.

Or maybe you aren't feeling even quite that desperate yet. You just have a gnawing, nagging sense inside that something is missing in your spiritual journey with Christ. The colors of your spiritual life are not quite as vivid as they used to be. You're not about to throw in the towel, but you have to admit you're tired. Slipping away unnoticed from the things of God for a while is not looking like too bad an option right now.

If you are in any of these spots right now or you know somebody who is, welcome to the body of Christ. I've been in these places and everywhere in between. It's no fun. The audience that Jesus was speaking to in Matthew 11:28–30 was probably filled with people like this. Jesus understands what we're going through and He offers us rest.

The *third* thing that strikes me from this passage is that Jesus isn't inviting us to come to Him for some good advice and then be sent on our way with "Good luck! Hope this works out for you!" parting words. He is beckoning us into an ongoing relationship... a walk together.

The imagery that Jesus was using was of a yoke made of wood that was draped over the shoulders of a team of oxen. Typically, a young, immature ox would be yoked with a mature, seasoned ox so the younger one could learn. In order for that younger ox to learn, it had to walk with the veteran, keeping in step with him, following his lead... not forging ahead in self-willed zeal, but not dragging its heels in stubborn resistance either.

Jesus' words were an invitation to a walk that accomplished useful work, not a God-given ticket to passivity and lazy inactivity.

I think you get the picture.

Jesus invites us to walk with Him, learning from Him, following His lead. When we live that way – rather than feeling like we are on our own, trying to live life by our own wits and good intentions and standards – we find rest for our souls. You can breathe a deep sigh of relief knowing it is not all up to you. It's up to Him to lead; your responsibility is to follow.

The choice is clear. Either we stay weary and heavy-laden or we surrender to Jesus' leadership, walking by His wisdom and power, and in so doing find that his yoke is easy and His burden is light.

Sounds like a no-brainer to me.

I conclude today's devotional with one of my favorite meditations on this amazing opportunity to experience rest in the grace of Jesus:

> When I meditated on the word "Guidance," I kept seeing the word "dance" at the end of it. I remember reading that doing God's will is a lot like dancing. When two people try to lead, nothing feels right. The movement doesn't flow with the music, and everything is quite uncomfortable and jerky. When one person relaxes and lets the other lead, both begin to flow with the music. One gives gentle cues, perhaps with a nudge to the back or by pressing lightly in one direction or another. It's as if two become one, moving beautifully together. The dance takes surrender, willingness and attentiveness from one person and gentle guidance and skill from the other. When I saw the letter "G" in "Guidance", I thought of God, followed by "u" and "I". And it hit me: "God, You (u) and I (i) dance." This statement is what guidance means to me. As I lowered my head, I became willing to trust that I would get guidance for my life. Once again, I became willing to let God lead.[9]

The "grace-rest" life is letting God lead. Jesus invites all who are weary and burdened to the dance. You will find rest for your soul. He will gently and humbly guide you in paths of righteousness for His name's sake. Will you accept His invitation?

A THOUGHT TO CHEW ON

The "grace-rest" life is to cease striving to make life work in our own strength and wisdom, and instead trusting in and walking with the Strong, Wise One... letting Him lead.

A TRUTH TO REMEMBER

"For the one who has entered His rest has himself also rested from his works, as God did from His" (Hebrews 4:10).

A QUESTION TO MULL OVER

Have you taken Jesus' easy, light yoke upon you and are you letting Him lead you in life or are you still wrestling with Him to maintain control of your own life? If the latter is the case, what is still keeping you from entering into the "grace-rest" life?

TALKING IT OVER WITH GOD

Dear Father, it seems so much easier to try and come up with a formula or list of "dos" and "don'ts" in order to gauge and control my spiritual life. But I guess that's the problem, isn't it? I want to control things. It is much harder, it seems, to surrender and relinquish control of my life to someone else... even Jesus. And yet His invitation is intriguing and His promise of rest for my soul sure sounds good. After all the stress and anxiety and cluttered, confused thoughts, I could use some rest.

Please continue to wear down my resistance so that I will take You up on Your offer… sooner rather than later. I can tell that I'm coming closer to the place of surrender but maybe I'm still afraid of what is on the other side of that decision. I feel a bit like Peter being encouraged to come out on the water to walk there with Jesus. It seems like a crazy thing to do, except for the fact that Jesus is the One doing the inviting. I guess regardless of what else I will find on the other side of the door of surrender, I know I will find Jesus and He promises me rest. I will need Your strength, Lord, so that when I see the wind and waves I don't get scared. Thanks for the chance to walk with You. Amen.

Day 37: Grace People

Hopefully yesterday's devotional began to give you a taste of what the "grace-rest" life is all about. If grace is God freely giving us what we don't deserve, what we can't come up with on our own and what we desperately need, then the "grace-rest" life is trusting in, resting in the fact that He will indeed do that… provide us with all the grace we need to live life His way.

The "grace-rest" life, though free from the shackles of rigid religious rules, is by no means a life of just sitting around waiting for Christ's return or something. It is an active life that requires us to step out of our comfort zones and follow Jesus in the dance… wherever He decides to lead. You need to be prepared for some unexpected twists, turns and spins! Let me tell you about one that just happened.

God has a sense of humor. I'm convinced of it. Now I don't mean that I think God the Father sits on His throne cracking jokes all day long. And I certainly don't think there is anything remotely like angelic canned laughter up in heaven. But some of the things the Lord does and the timing of them just makes me smile, shake my head and even chuckle a bit.

Today was one of those times. Let me put today into a helpful context.

Yesterday in our church's worship service, our pastor preached on the parable of the Good Samaritan. You might recall that Jesus told that story because of a man who wanted to justify himself before the Lord. The guy was pretty proud of how he had kept the commandments and when Jesus encouraged him to go and love his neighbor as himself, the man asked, "And who is my neighbor?" (Luke 10:27–29). Talk about giving the Lord an opening!

Jesus then proceeded to tell one of his patented stories

that completely blew away the listeners. In summary, the story goes like this. After a man had been robbed and beaten and left for dead on the road from Jerusalem to Jericho, both a priest and a Levite walked around the poor fellow and did nothing to help him. But, to the complete shock of the listeners, in Jesus' tale a Samaritan (despised by the Jews) became the hero. He went out of his way to generously help the guy in need, even promising to come back and check on the poor man later and take care of any additional expenses.

"Which of these three do you think proved to be a neighbor to the man who fell into the robbers' hands?" Jesus asked.

With his mouth hanging open and his eyes bugging out, I'm sure, the self-justifying man said, "The one who showed mercy toward him."

"Go and do the same," Jesus concluded.

Interesting turn of the conversation by Jesus, don't you think? The one seeking to justify himself wanted to know who his neighbor was. Jesus was more concerned about his listener being a good neighbor. In other words, Jesus was teaching him not to be so concerned with figuring out who he should help or shouldn't help. But rather, he should be a person with a good and gracious heart who would naturally – or rather, supernaturally – help the people in need that he encountered. People of grace are like that. They genuinely care for people, even strangers, and take pity on those in need.

Here's where God's sense of humor comes in. At the end of my pastor's sermon, he must have repeated Jesus' words, "Go and do the same" at least three or four times. And, being a good Christian, I said, "Yes, Lord, I will."

This morning while I was taking part of a day off, getting ready to enjoy a peaceful time with the Lord, the phone rang. A friend of mine had two doctor's appointments this morning and his mother (afraid of the impending bad weather) didn't want to take him to the appointments as planned. The phone call came with my friend desperate for a ride, since he, being legally blind, couldn't drive himself.

After first having to get over my irritation with the fearful mother, I agreed to help him.

The first appointment was coming up really quickly and I also had to first drop my wife, Shirley, off at work. Could I make it in time? Missing the doctor's appointment would have been very problematic for my friend and I had to get him there by 9:10 a.m. in order to make it on time.

Admittedly being a bit liberal with the speed limits, with a sigh of relief, I pulled up to the front of the doctor's office (thanks to the Lord providing some very helpful green traffic lights!) at 9:08.

The appointments and travel ended up taking all my "morning off," but I had to smile. I knew what God was up to. He was checking out how sincere I was yesterday in church when I made the commitment to be a good neighbor. God's serious sense of humor strikes again.

My friend's doctor appointments went really well, by the way (he is diabetic), and he was really grateful for the ride. I even got to talk about God's love and grace to a boy in one of the waiting rooms. He was so curious about what I was doing with my laptop that he couldn't resist asking me. And I happened to be editing this book! So I told him all about it.

When we enter into the "grace-rest" life, we become what I call "grace people"… people who have entered into the rest of Jesus by surrendering to His will and walking by faith in His grace, knowing that He is fully committed to taking care of all our needs. And when we are resting securely in the knowledge that God is fully committed to taking care of our needs, we are freed up to concern ourselves with meeting the needs of others.

I really want to be a grace person... living a life of gratefully loving God and eagerly, lovingly helping others... and I know God wants me to be that way, too. But have you ever noticed how being grace people requires our willingness to be inconvenienced?

Those who live their lives under a performance-based, law standard are usually rigid and inflexible. They get really irritated and bent out of shape when something disrupts their neatly controlled world. To be a grace person, you have to give up everything to God's control... including your time, your energy, your money and your convenience... to allow the Lord to interrupt your world and intersect your grace life with grace-needy people. If you're not used to it, it can seem like a real pain. But when you learn to go with the flow of what God is up to, it can be a real adventure of living in love. I'm still learning, as I discovered this morning.

Paul was teaching his spiritual child, Timothy, how to be a grace person. He told him, "You therefore, my son, be strong in the grace that is in Christ Jesus" (2 Timothy 2:1).

A wise Bible teacher used to say, "When you see the word 'therefore' you need to ask what the 'therefore' is there for." So let's backtrack slightly and read the end of chapter 1:

> You are aware of the fact that all who are in Asia
> turned away from me, among whom are Phygelus
> and Hermogenes. The Lord grant mercy to the house
> of Onesiphorus, for he often refreshed me and was
> not ashamed of my chains; but when he was in Rome,
> he eagerly searched for me and found me – the Lord
> grant to him to find mercy from the Lord on that day –
> and you know very well what services he rendered at
> Ephesus.
>
> 2 Timothy 1:15–18

Sadly, Paul found himself surrounded by non-grace people who rejected him, including two guys that I like to refer to as "Fidgety" and "Homogenized." But Onesiphorus was different. He was a grace person. I think there are at least three things about grace people that Paul was wanting to teach Tim – and us – from the life of Onesiphorus.

First, grace people are *refreshing*. Onesiphorus often refreshed Paul. Grace people are like that. Non-grace people, on the other hand, tend to drain the life out of you. They are stress-carriers who sweat the small stuff and spread their anxiety to others. Grace people pour life into you rather than drain energy out of you. They are an encouragement.

Second, grace people are *accepting*. No matter what condition you are in, whether self-inflicted or not, they still love you and meet you where you are in life. Being in prison was not a badge of honor in Paul's day any more than it is today, but that didn't matter to Onesiphorus. He came with grace to one who was in disgrace.

Third, grace people are *relational*. Those who are non-grace people tend to value perfection more than people, laws more than love and rules rather than relationships. Onesiphorus sought after Paul, eagerly, and wasn't content until he found him. Rome was a big place and he couldn't just Google "Paul in Roman prison" and immediately know his whereabouts. It took some time and energy to find him, and he did, because he loved Paul. And this clearly was this grace person's lifestyle, as Paul reminded Timothy of how Onesiphorus had helped him in Ephesus.

So the exhortation from Paul to Timothy is ours as well: "You therefore, my son [or daughter], be strong in the grace that is in Christ Jesus" (2 Timothy 2:1).

Tomorrow we'll take a look at how God brings us to the point of being willing to surrender and enter the "grace-rest life", becoming fruitful like Onesiphorus... strong in grace and being refreshing, accepting, relational people.

A THOUGHT TO CHEW ON

Being a grace person requires a willingness to be inconvenienced.

A TRUTH TO REMEMBER

"You therefore, my son, be strong in the grace that is in Christ Jesus" (2 Timothy 2:1).

A QUESTION TO MULL OVER

Would people describe you as a refreshing, accepting, relational person? If not, what is hindering you from being a grace person?

TALKING IT OVER WITH GOD

Dear heavenly Father, it has been said that you can tell the depth of a man's faith by looking at his checkbook and his calendar. How then can you tell the depth of a man's grace? How can I know if I am growing strong in the grace that is in Christ Jesus? I want to be someone who is known for being refreshing, accepting and relational... not draining, critical, rejecting and unwilling to be inconvenienced to help others in need.

What are the obstacles that still remain in my life that keep me from being full of grace and truth like the Lord Jesus? Would you please open up my eyes in the days ahead so that the un-gracious things in me and the dis-graceful qualities I have are chipped away like the sharp and rough edges off a sculptor's masterpiece. Amen.

Day 38: It's Not That Easy

I was having one of those totally-honest-and-intimate-with-God talks that makes following Jesus really real. Maybe you know what I mean. There are lots of times when you know He's there but the distance between your finite life and His infinite Presence seems nearly impossible to bridge. You read the Bible and pray and you know it is benefitting you at some level, but the heart-to-heart connection with the Lord somehow seems to be missing. This was not one of those times. For whatever reason, I not only knew by faith that He was with me and in me, I could just sense it with every fiber of my being. It made me hungry for heaven.

Wanting to let the Lord know in a special way that I wanted Him to have all of me, I prayed a very sincere prayer. It went something like this:

"Lord, I love You and I want to follow You with all that I am. I know that there is still so much in me that needs to go, so would You please deliver me from everything in my life that displeases You? I want it gone. I really mean it, Lord. Please take it all away."

I waited silently for the Lord to do a powerful new work in my life. I fully expected to be ushered into some higher and deeper echelon of spirituality at that moment. It wasn't long until I sensed the gentle, Fatherly voice of God ministering deep in my heart:

"My son, it's not that easy."

Those were not the words I was hoping to hear, but as the Lord spoke them to me, I knew they were the truth.

What did He mean?

Well, to be perfectly honest, this may come across at first glance as pretty lousy news, but it is extremely important and actually very good news. First of all, God is committed to making us like Christ. That is His will. Second, He is filled with joy when His sons and daughters want to walk with Him in what we call the "grace-rest" or abiding life. Third, the process of coming to the place of yielding to His Presence and walking in grace is not an easy one. In fact, it is typically quite difficult and often painful. Most likely that is why so few get there.

Not surprisingly, the apostle Paul wrote from firsthand experience about this process of bringing us to the point of surrendering control and allowing Christ to be our life:

> But we have this treasure in earthen vessels, so that the surpassing greatness of the power will be of God and not from ourselves; we are afflicted in every way, but not crushed; perplexed, but not despairing; persecuted, but not forsaken; struck down, but not destroyed; always carrying about in the body the dying of Jesus, so that the life of Jesus also may be manifested in our body. For we who live are constantly being delivered over to death for Jesus' sake, so that the life of Jesus also may be manifested in our mortal flesh. So death works in us, but life in you.
>
> 2 Corinthians 4:7–12

I know this is pretty heavy. That's why I waited until nearly the end of this devotional to break this news to you. Believe me, I wish I could tell you that if you just go to a certain worship or revival service, sing a lot of great songs, hear a stirring message that challenges you to serve Christ with all your heart, and you shout a hearty "Amen!" then that would be it.

My brother or sister, it's not that easy.

Why not?

From Paul's letter quoted above, the answer seems to be that in order for us to enter into this grace-rest life of having the life of Christ powerfully at work in and through us, something has to happen first. And that something is death.

Like I said, at first glance this is not exciting news. After all, who wants to die?

The apostle listed off a number of experiences he was undergoing that were decidedly unpleasant: being afflicted, perplexed, persecuted and struck down. He was talking about life experiences where things go wrong and you feel enormous pressure. You don't know what to do and time is running out. The whole world seems to be ganging up on you and life caves in around you. You lose your job or your health or your savings or your reputation. Maybe all of the above. Your world just seems to come crashing down and no amount of praying, pleading, manipulating or problem solving serves to extricate you from the feeling of being hunted and trapped. It seems like death. And so it is.

But death isn't the end.

The good news is that just as Christ's death on the cross wasn't the end of the story, so neither is our painful dying to all that we cling to for life, security and happiness apart from Christ.

There is resurrection.

Remembering that life follows death in God's kingdom is what keeps you from going crazy when life in this world plays hardball with you. Somehow Paul was able to keep from being crushed and despairing, knowing that God would never forsake him. He was hurting but he was still alive. He was dying to his own self-reliant ways on the inside but he was watching Christ's resurrection life poured outside to others through his broken and contrite heart.

And that is a good thing... a very good thing.

If you have been in Christ for a while, you probably have already experienced what I'm talking about. In fact, the Bible says that all true children of God will go through this process. Hebrews 12:5–7 says:

> "My son, do not regard lightly the discipline of the LORD, nor faint when you are reproved by Him; for those whom the LORD loves He disciplines, and He scourges every son whom He receives." It is for discipline that you endure; God deals with you as with sons; for what son is there whom his father does not discipline?

Did you catch that? God disciplines us, not out of anger or hatred or with some nasty desire to make us miserable, but out of His love. In fact, later in that chapter, the writer of Hebrews says, "but He [God] disciplines us for our good, so that we may share His holiness" (Hebrews 12:10).

2 Corinthians calls it "the dying of Jesus" so that His life will show through us. Hebrews 12 calls it "the discipline of the Lord", given in love for our good that we may share His holiness. John 15 calls it "pruning" so that we may bear more fruit (verse 2).

Is it easy? No.

Is it fun? Certainly not. Hebrews 12:11 says, "All discipline for the moment seems not to be joyful, but sorrowful…"

Is it worth it? Ah… that is the question that each of us must answer.

A THOUGHT TO CHEW ON

It's not that easy.

A TRUTH TO REMEMBER

"For those whom the LORD loves He disciplines…" (Hebrews 12:6).

A QUESTION TO MULL OVER

Think of a time when things in life were tough beyond your ability to change them. How did you respond? Looking back over that time, can you now see how the Lord used it for your good? Why or why not?

TALKING IT OVER WITH GOD

Dear loving Father, the path to living the grace-rest life is not an easy one, is it? Words like "pruning," "discipline," and "dying" indicate one thing in my mind… pain. There's a part of me that wonders how Your intentional "treatment" of pain can be a good thing, an act of love. But then I think about things like athletic training, medical surgery and physical therapy… times of life that involve pain for the purpose of strengthening and healing… and I am reminded that not everything that hurts, harms.

Are the patterns in my life of self-centered, self-sufficient living buried so deep and intertwined in my soul so thoroughly that it takes such radical measures to root them out? It seems that way. If Your love means that I will not escape discipline, then please grant me the grace to endure it, even though I know I won't enjoy it. I know deep down in my heart that it is worth it all. Amen.

Day 39: Living the "Grace-Rest" Life

Abiding in or "making your home" in Christ is in essence what the "grace-rest" life is all about. He is in us and we are in Him. There is a very real but very mysterious union between us. It is in some ways like plugging a lamp into the electric outlet. Nothing appears different between a lamp that is plugged in and a lamp that is not plugged in until you turn on the plugged-in lamp. Then suddenly the light comes on and brightens and cheers the whole room because it is connected to this immense power grid that you cannot see. Coming to Christ as Savior is like plugging in the lamp and entering into the "grace-rest" life is like deciding to turn on that lamp and allowing our light – really His light – to shine through us to a dark world.

Jesus in John 15 used the analogy of growing grapes to explain it. He is the Vine and we are the branches. Allowing His life to pour into us like the nourishment that comes through the grapevine into the branch so it can bear fruit is what life in Christ is all about. As I said before, it is what life is meant to be.

I believe there are two very important but distinct parts of living the "grace-rest" life of abiding in Christ. The first part is what we have been talking about so far this week... coming to the point of brokenness and giving up living life in our own strength and self-will and surrendering to Christ as our Lord and Life. That is what Paul had in mind when he wrote:

> Therefore I urge you, brethren, by the mercies of
> God, to present your bodies a living and holy sacrifice,
> acceptable to God, which is your spiritual service
> of worship.

Romans 12:1

It is interesting that this surrender is of our *bodies*. This is simply because everything we do in this world, whether good or evil, involves our bodies.

First, we surrender our brains (which means our minds, including all our memories, hopes, dreams, plans, knowledge, wisdom, attitudes, emotions, and so on) to Him. We make the decision to set our minds on what is true, honorable, right, pure, lovely, of good repute, excellent, and worthy of praise (Philippians 4:8).

Notice that God doesn't legalistically give us the list of the "good, bad and ugly" books, magazines, films, TV shows, music, computer games, websites and so on for us to rigidly follow. The list would be outdated before it was even published anyway! But God gives us principles by which we can discern with His wisdom what to be part of and what to stay away from.

We surrender our eyes and ears so that we look upon the things and listen to the things that will honor Him and benefit us.

We surrender our mouths so that "no unwholesome word proceeds from your mouth, but only such a word as is good for edification according to the need of the moment, so that it will give grace to those who hear" (Ephesians 4:29).

We surrender our hands – all that we touch and do – so that what we do is to the glory of God (1 Corinthians 10:31). We surrender our feet – all the places where we go. It is no longer "my will" but "Thy will" be done.

And so on. You get the picture.

Every place where you surrender control, invite the presence and power of the Holy Spirit to fill that empty place. And by so doing you will enter, by faith, into the "grace-rest" life of abiding in Christ.

But how do you stay there? How do you grow in the

grace and knowledge of our Lord and Savior Jesus Christ (2 Peter 3:18)? How do you become strong in the grace that is in Christ Jesus (2 Timothy 2:1)?

That brings us to the second part of the "grace-rest" life, once we have chosen to enter that place of surrender. Part two involves living day by day in an abiding relationship with Jesus.

It's kind of like being married. I remember the day, August 12, 1989, when I said "I do" to Shirley Grace. At that point I was legally married, with the marriage consummated soon after. On August 13, 1989 as we took off for our honeymoon in Jamaica, we could not have been more married.

The wedding ceremony is like part one of this "grace-rest" life. After I went through all my own mental and emotional gymnastics about getting married or not getting married, I surrendered to the call to marriage and entered into this relationship with Shirley… by faith.

But to be perfectly honest, at first, being married seemed a bit awkward. It felt weird to me to have to tell her where I was going. I couldn't just take off on my own anymore. That didn't feel like freedom. It took some time to get comfortable living together. I had to share my money with her! That didn't seem fair. It took some time also to get comfortable sleeping together. I found out she snored! Hey, that wasn't in the contract, was it? (To be fair, she says I make a weird puffing noise when I sleep.)

If you're married, you know what I'm talking about. It is one thing to be married. It is quite another thing to learn how to live married and to enjoy the oneness and freedom of that union.

It's the same thing with our relationship with Christ. It takes time to get to know each other and to start feeling comfortable together. Of course, He has no problem understanding and relating to us… all the learning and growth is on our side!

Now I could proceed to rattle off the ten things that you should do to abide in Christ and grow in grace, and that would work just about as well as somebody rattling off the ten things that I should do to get to know Shirley better. I mean, there would be some benefit but everyone's relationship with Christ, just like every marriage relationship, is different.

That's one of the really beautiful and adventurous things about entering into the "grace-rest" life of abiding in Christ. You are surrendering to the infinitely creative Creator of the universe who knows you inside and out and who understands exactly how to relate to you and how you were designed to relate to Him!

One thing is clearly important. You and Jesus need to spend time together. You will want to hear what He has to say to you and He is eagerly waiting to hear what you have to say to Him. As you grow in your love for Him and watch all the amazing ways that He provides for you and protects you, you won't be able to keep from praising and worshipping Him.

If you tend toward the very active, busy, "task oriented" side of life, and all this waiting around and listening seems problematic to you, the following story from Jesus' life might be helpful.

Now as they were traveling along, He entered a village; and a woman named Martha welcomed Him into her home. She had a sister called Mary, who was seated at the Lord's feet, listening to His word. But Martha was distracted with all her preparations; and she came up to Him and said, "Lord, do You not care that my sister has left me to do all the serving alone? Then tell her to help me." But the Lord answered and said to her, "Martha, Martha, you are worried and bothered about so many

> things; but only one thing is necessary, for Mary has
> chosen the good part, which shall not be taken away
> from her."

Luke 10:38–42

Mary was listening to the word of God spoken by Jesus, the Word of God Himself. Without Jesus being physically around to teach us, reading His word, the Bible, is the best way to hear from Him now. And prayer is our primary means of talking with Him. You will have lots of questions to ask Him about how to live life. He has all the answers. Turn your questions into prayers and wait expectantly for Him to lead and direct your steps.

Though Jesus will most certainly guide you to walk in the good works that He has created for you to do (Ephesians 2:10), don't fall into the trap that Martha did... being so busy serving Jesus that you miss out on seeking Him.

Undergirding all this relationship with Jesus in the "grace-rest" life is the knowledge that in Christ you are unconditionally and perfectly loved, totally accepted, completely secure and immeasurably significant. You can't go back to these truths too often!

We posed the question yesterday as to whether all this is really worth it. And what I said is true. Every one of us needs to wrestle with that question and come up with our own answer. But I decided to be a little more gracious and not just leave you hanging. We'll finish up our forty days tomorrow by providing some thoughts that may help you answer that question.

A THOUGHT TO CHEW ON

Once we enter into the "grace-rest" life, we then need to learn how to grow in grace, abiding in Christ.

A TRUTH TO REMEMBER

"… but only one thing is necessary, for Mary has chosen the good part, which shall not be taken from her" (Luke 10:42).

A QUESTION TO MULL OVER

What are some creative ways you can think of to get to know Jesus better and grow in His grace? If you are struggling, ask God to help you. Think of things that give you a sense of joy and freedom rather than a sense of obligation or duty.

TALKING IT OVER WITH GOD

Gracious Father, I just want to take a moment to say "Thank You."

Thank You for Your patience with me. Thank You for Your love that draws me. Thank You for all Your mercies that let me know that surrendering to You is the right and safe thing to do. Thank You for forgiving me and giving me life when I did not deserve that. In fact, I deserved the exact opposite. Thank You for sending Jesus when You would have been perfectly just to let us rot here on earth in our rebellion and sin. Thank You for giving me the Holy Spirit who is changing me slowly but surely into a "grace person."

Sometimes I can't believe all this is real and that I'm not going to wake up disappointed one day to discover this was all just a dream. No. You are real and heaven is real and everything good that You are doing in my life is really real, too. Amazing grace! Thank You. Amen.

Day 40: Is It All Really Worth It?

As we finish up these forty days of looking at God's amazing grace, it is still possible you might be asking the question – if not out loud, then perhaps deep in your heart – "Is walking with Jesus really worth it? Is the grace-rest life of surrender to Christ and abiding in Him worth all the chiseling the Lord has to do in our lives to get us to that place of humility and keep us there?"

If you are asking that very honest question, it could be that you are going through a really difficult period in your life right now. The concept of suffering is not at all theoretical for you but is the unwelcome reality that rushes to greet you in the morning with its gut-twisting pain, and is your last conscious thought as you fitfully drop off to sleep somewhere in the night… assuming you are able to sleep at all.

If that is your situation right now, I sincerely hope that God has brought some measure of consolation to you in the pages of this devotional. In the midst of pain it is wise to remember that God remains good and, yes, He is gracious. It is easy to forget that there is still vivid color in the world when life drones on in listless gray.

And I pray you are not going through this time of testing alone. Even Jesus took Peter, James and John with Him to the Garden of Gethsemane for His hour of unimaginable anguish, even though the three amigos literally fell asleep on the job of being there for Him.

Or it could be you are asking this chapter's question out of nervous curiosity. You are relatively new to this Christian stuff and I scared you a little bit back in Day 38. If that happened, sorry. That wasn't my intention at all. I was just trying to help a newer passenger on this rugged journey with Jesus get prepared for some rough air up ahead. Can you tell

I am writing this on an airline flight?

The question is still on the table. Is it all really worth it?

Certainly, Satan would loudly hiss his answer in our minds that God is cruel and uncaring and cold and even abusive and so, he says, "You are way better off living on your own, taking care of yourself, watching your own back. You can't really trust God to have your best interests at heart." I suspect he was the one pulling the strings on Job's wife's vocal chords when, after that poor man lost all that was dear to him, she cried out, "Do you still hold fast your integrity? Curse God and die!" (Job 2:9).

Did you ever wonder why Satan did not destroy her, because he had permission to do so. Sadly, it was likely because he knew he could cause Job more suffering by letting her live.

Job's courageous words in the midst of almost unbelievable pain pierced through the demonic darkness and give light to us as well:

> "You speak as one of the foolish women speaks. Shall we indeed accept good from God and not accept adversity?" In all this Job did not sin with his lips.
>
> Job 2:10

One of the things (and there are many!) that is instructive about the book of Job is that it is clear the man did not have a clue while he was going through his suffering why it was happening. God apparently later revealed to him that he was part of a cosmic spiritual battle between the devil and Himself, and in order for evil to be defeated, Job had to be, at least temporarily, kept in the dark concerning the "Why?" question.

And this is why suffering can be so hard. Our lives are a full-length movie or a long novel. God is the Producer or the Author of the story and we are the leading character in it. Our suffering is like a scene from the film or a page or chapter from the book. If we were to look at that picture or read those words outside of their full context, without knowing the end of the story, we could easily despair. Suffering ultimately makes no sense apart from God, and many times we struggle with making sense of it even when we *are* following God.

But as difficult as the way of Jesus can be, in the end, it is better to know God than to know *why*.

As I myself wrestle with this chapter's question, it occurs to me that the people who can give the best answer to it are not those in the midst of suffering, but those who have come through it. It is better to ask a mother holding her newborn in her arms if the pain was worth it rather than ask that same dear woman several hours earlier in the midst of an excruciating contraction.

As a man, I cannot experience those extremes of childbirth. But as a husband and father I have seen them both. And perhaps, in that stark contrast, the answer to today's question can be found.

Certainly there has been no one who has experienced more sorrow and suffering than our Lord Jesus, and yet…

… let us run with endurance the race that is set before us, fixing our eyes on Jesus, the author and perfecter of faith, who for the joy set before Him endured the cross, despising the shame, and has sat down at the right hand of the throne of God.

For consider Him who has endured such hostility by sinners against Himself, so that you will not grow weary and lose heart.

Hebrews 12:1a–3

There it is. Did you see it? It's easy to skip over the word… joy. Joy is what gives us the ability to endure suffering. There are at least six aspects of joy that come in the midst of and as a result of our pain. Entire books have been written about suffering, but we only have time here to quickly tap these profound subjects on the shoulder.

What kind of joy can be found in the midst of pain?

First, there is the joy of nearness to God, in whose presence is the fullness of joy (Psalm 16:11). C. S. Lewis knew what he was talking about in *The Problem of Pain* when he wrote:

> We can even ignore pleasure. But pain insists upon
> being attended to. God whispers to us in our pleasures,
> speaks in our conscience, but shouts in our pains: it is
> his megaphone to a deaf world.

Those who have been through intense suffering and experienced the uncanny closeness of God in the midst of that pain are quick to say that they would not have missed that season of life for anything. Only those who have walked that way know the truth of their testimony.

Second, there is the joy that comes after the suffering as we are made more like Christ. Hebrews 12:11 says:

> All discipline for the moment seems not to be joyful,
> but sorrowful; yet to those who have been trained by it,
> afterwards it yields the peaceful fruit of righteousness.

For those who long to enter into the "grace-rest" life, this is what it is all about. There is no cost that those with a seeking heart will not bear to become like their Lord.

Third, one can find the joy of watching God powerfully touch the lives of those around us as we patiently endure the suffering He has ordained for us. The apostle Paul spoke of the beauty of this mysterious life-giving dynamic when he wrote:

> ... always carrying about in the body the dying of Jesus, so that the life of Jesus also may be manifested in our body. For we who live are constantly being delivered over to death for Jesus' sake, so that the life of Jesus also may be manifested in our mortal flesh. So death works in us, but life in you.
>
> 2 Corinthians 4:10–12

Fourth, there is also the joy of experiencing the honor of suffering for the name of Christ. After the apostles had been arrested and ordered by the Jewish Council not to preach about Jesus any more, the Jewish leaders flogged them and then let them go. Amazingly, while most of us would have been calling 911 to be taken by ambulance to the ER, the apostles "went on their way... rejoicing that they had been considered worthy to suffer shame for His [Jesus'] name" (Acts 5:41).

Fifth, there is the prospect of joy in the thrill of experiencing the direct intervention of God in the midst of suffering... either in being healed, being rescued or even in being ushered into eternity. Peter wrote:

> After you have suffered for a little while, the God of all grace, who called you to His eternal glory in Christ, will Himself perfect, confirm, strengthen and establish you. To Him be dominion forever and ever. Amen.
>
> 1 Peter 5:10–11

Sixth (and I am sure there are many more that could be mentioned), we cannot forget the joy of seeing Jesus face to face and being commended by Him for a life well lived:

His master said to him, "Well done, good and faithful
slave. You were faithful with a few things, I will put
you in charge of many things; enter into the joy of your
master."

Matthew 25:21

This is the one that truly only those who have passed through
this life of suffering and yet have chosen to walk with Christ,
abiding in Him in the "grace-rest" life, can testify about. Paul,
who suffered greatly and yet chose to walk with Christ, was
inspired to give us these words to sustain, strengthen and
encourage us during the dark days:

For I consider that the sufferings of this present time are
not worthy to be compared with the glory that is to be
revealed to us.

Romans 8:18

And I believe him.

So here we are at the end of this brief discovery of and journey
in grace. We will end this last day differently from the other
thirty-nine. We will still have a place for "A thought to chew
on," "A truth to remember," and "Talking it over with God,"
but I am leaving them blank for you to fill in. It will be good
for you to express your heart here, unprompted by me.

I guess what I'm saying is that, as we talked about at the
beginning, it is time to decide whether to waddle or to fly. The
invitation from Jesus to change is here. Will you accept it?

As for "A question to mull over," it is the same one that
Jesus asked the apostles after He had given a hard teaching
and many of His disciples went away and stopped walking
with Him:

So Jesus said to the twelve, "You do not want to go away also, do you?"

John 6:66–67

A searching question, don't you think?

My earnest prayer and hope is that you would heartily answer with the apostle Peter:

Lord, to whom shall we go? You have words of eternal life. We have believed and have come to know that You are the Holy One of God.

John 6:68–69

That same Peter, years later, in concluding his first inspired letter to his brothers and sisters in Christ who were suffering and scattered throughout Asia, wrote in 1 Peter 5:12:

Through Silvanus, our faithful brother (for so I regard him), I have written to you briefly, exhorting and testifying that this is the true grace of God. Stand firm in it!

That is what I have tried to do during these forty days, though obviously the only inspired part of this book is what has been quoted from God's word.

May the Lord's grace and peace be with you as you continue growing strong in the grace that is in Christ Jesus. This is the true grace of God. Stand firm in it!

A THOUGHT TO CHEW ON

A TRUTH TO REMEMBER

TALKING IT OVER WITH GOD

Amen.

Final Words

In Christ, we are the totally undeserved but unbelievably privileged beneficiaries of God's amazing grace. Ephesians 1:8 uses the word "lavished" to describe God pouring out His grace generously, bountifully, exuberantly, and extravagantly on us. It's not a drizzle; it's a deluge. And for these forty days I have sought to grab you by the hand, pull you out of the cave of dry, religious dreariness and joyfully run with you through the rain.

Now that the forty days of "rain" are over (hmm, why am I suddenly thinking about Noah and a bunch of animals on a smelly boat…), what's next?

I hope you are asking that question. It's the right question to ask.

What *is* next? More grace. John 1:16 says of Jesus, "For of His fullness we have all received, and grace upon grace." Grace upon grace upon grace upon… It never stops. And we happily will spend the rest of our days on earth, and an eternity in heaven, watching with wide-eyed amazement the wonders of God and His goodness to us, "to the praise of the glory of His grace, which He freely bestowed on us in the Beloved [Jesus]" (Ephesians 1:6).

OK, that's great, but is there anything else? As a matter of fact there is. Something actually quite huge.

Just as somewhere, somehow the message of God's grace in truth was brought to you and me, we have the amazing opportunity to spread this good news to others who have not yet come out of their caves. Most don't even realize there's anywhere else to live. Paul talked about the spread of the gospel in Colossians 1:3–6:

We give thanks to God, the Father of our Lord Jesus Christ, praying always for you, since we heard of your faith in Christ Jesus and the love which you have for all the saints; because of the hope laid up for you in heaven, of which you previously heard in the word of truth, the gospel which has come to you, just as in all the world also it is constantly bearing fruit and increasing, even as it has been doing in you also since the day you heard of it and understood the grace of God in truth...

You see, God is up to something and it is so big that we struggle to get our minds around it. He is bringing time and life and everything on this planet and beyond to a staggering conclusion. Despite how little most people think about Jesus, especially here in the West, this is all going to change. Right after the apostle Paul talked about how God has lavished grace on us, he wrote:

In all wisdom and insight He made known to us the mystery of His will, according to His kind intention which He purposed in Him [Christ] with a view to an administration suitable to the fullness of the times, that is, the summing up of all things in Christ, things in the heavens and things on the earth.

Ephesians 1:8b–10

One day, Jesus will be center stage in the universe. Everything will point to Him. Every mind will be thinking about Him. Every mouth will be talking about Him. Every heart will wrestle with what to do with Him. Every person will be compelled to face Him. He will be revealed in such stunning glory that every jaw will drop at His appearing.

That time is coming.

So what is our role between now and then? Basically,

we are to be like the newsboy on the street proclaiming the latest story: *Extra! Extra! Read all about it!* Though we may not literally be yelling in the street (though God *could* call us to do that!), I think you get the point.

We have been given grace-news, not to keep to ourselves, but to share, to pass on to others. This is exciting news – in fact, *the most exciting news!* You see, there are people all around us to whom God wants to freely give something they don't deserve and cannot come up with on their own, but desperately need – the gospel.

And you and I get to tell them. I'm sure the angels wish they had that job, but their role is actually to provide behind-the-scenes tactical support as we do it.

Incredible grace… given to us to pass on to others. It's kind of like a relay race. Jesus first brought the good news and passed the baton to the apostles who passed it on to others who passed it down to still others and eventually it came to you and me. That race isn't finished yet, and now it's our turn to pass this life-giving message of God's grace on to others.

Run well!

Therefore, since we have so great a cloud of witnesses surrounding us, let us also lay aside every encumbrance and the sin which so easily entangles us, and let us run with endurance the race that is set before us, fixing our eyes on Jesus, the author and perfecter of faith, who for the joy set before Him endured the cross, despising the shame, and has sat down at the right hand of the throne of God.

For consider Him who has endured such hostility by sinners against Himself, so that you will not grow weary and lose heart.

Hebrews 12:1–3

Finally, it is good to know that, even though God's grace will never run out, but will take us to and through our final breath here on earth, there is a future grace that awaits us. It is the grace of eternity with our Lord Jesus, and is most assuredly ours in Christ, no matter what hardship and misery life on this planet throws at us. And in that future grace is where our hope must ultimately lie. The apostle Peter knew what he was talking about when he wrote:

> Therefore, prepare your minds for action, keep sober in spirit, fix your hope completely on the grace to be brought to you at the revelation of Jesus Christ.
>
> 1 Peter 1:13

Tough times are ahead for all of us. But for those of us in Christ those times are temporary and not worthy to be compared to the glory that will be revealed (Romans 8:18). How can I be so optimistic? Simply because Jesus promised to make all things new, and since He is on His throne in heaven and He is in charge and His words are trustworthy and true (Revelation 21:5), we can rest in them. You can rest in them.

> And I heard a loud voice from the throne, saying, "Behold, the tabernacle of God is among men, and He will dwell among them, and they shall be His people, and God Himself will be among them, and He will wipe away every tear from their eyes; and there will no longer be any death; there will no longer be any mourning, or crying, or pain; the first things have passed away."
>
> Revelation 21:3–4

The grace of the Lord Jesus be with all. Amen.

> Revelation 22:21

Notes

1. Greg Morris, "Why Waddle When You Can Fly!", *Leadership Dynamics* e-newsletter (www.leadershipdynamics@lb.bcentral. com).

2. Neil T. Anderson, Rich Miller and Paul Travis, *Breaking the Bondage of Legalism*, Eugene, OR: Harvest House Publishers, 2003, p. 29. Used by permission.

3. Adapted from Nena Benigno, "Sharing the Freedom of Forgiveness," in *People Reaching People*, Philippine Campus Crusade for Christ, vol. XI, no. 1, Sep. 1992, p. 7.

4. Kevin A. Miller, "I Don't Feel Like a Very Good Christian," *Discipleship Journal*, Issue 47, 1988, p. 6. Used with permission.

5. Anderson, Miller and Travis, *Breaking the Bondage of Legalism*, pp. 71–3.

6. Adapted from Don McMinn, *Spiritual Strongholds*, Oklahoma City, OK: NCM Press, 1993, pp. 73–4.

7. Adapted from www.top20fun.com/funny_jokes/4916.html

8. Anderson, Miller and Travis, *Breaking the Bondage of Legalism*, pp. 258–60.

9. Pauline Lamarre, "Asking for Guidance," as found on *Christian Women Today* website (http://archive.christianwomentoday.com/reflection/guidance.html).